Sent to the Principal

Sent to the Principal

Students Talk About Making High Schools Better

BY KATHLEEN CUSHMAN
and the students of What Kids Can Do

Foreword by DEBORAH MEIER

with contributions from high school principals
TERI SCHRADER

OLIVIA IFILL-LYNCH

LYNN HAINES-DODD

and a special report on Students as Allies
by BARBARA CERVONE

NEXT GENERATION PRESS

PROVIDENCE. RHODE ISLAND

Published in the United States of America by Next Generation Press
Printed in China by Kwong Fat Offset Printing Co. Ltd.
Distributed by National Book Network, Lanham, Maryland

ISBN 0-9762706-1-7

CIP data available

Book design by Sandra Delany

Next Generation Press, a not-for-profit book publisher, brings forward the voices and
views of adolescents on their own lives, learning, and work. With a particular focus on
youth without privilege, Next Generation Press raises awareness of young people as a
powerful force for social justice.

Next Generation Press, P.O. Box 603252, Providence, RI 02906
www.nextgenerationpress.org

10 9 8 7 6 5 4 3 2 1

*This book is dedicated
to students who speak their minds
and to leaders who listen*

Contents

Foreword

BY DEBORAH MEIER

S OMETHING NEW HAS CREPT UP UPON US: We are raising kids in the company of strangers at best, and mostly in the company of their peers. In human history, societies always took for granted that the closer the young came to adulthood, the more they kept company with adults. For us, it's the reverse. Even families are more and more estranged from the daily life and work of their adolescent offspring.

It won't work.

We need to hear each other, and not by just sending messages out into the void and hoping they will be read and made sense of. Powerful as this book is, it is above all a plea for each of us to listen in person, to reorganize the way we go about our lives and business to make space for face-to-face contact, ideally in a leisurely way.

The kids did not invent this new form of childhood and adolescence. The adult world designed it, hook, line and sinker. We have left teenagers open to a voracious advertising industry eager to part them from their money and well-trained to reach their hearts and minds to do so. How better to isolate them than in a peer community with so few ties to the larger world, and to those younger or older than themselves?

They therefore come to the school, as Kathleen Cushman reminds us, to see their friends. They "own the school" in a very different sense than we had in mind. In fact, how nice it would be if they did own it, in the positive sense of having a deep commitment to its goals and values.

But then we would need clearer and more compelling goals and values than the ones we now espouse. You come to school, young people hear from our system now, so you can make more money.

Their resistance, as this book reminds us, is not an altogether unhealthy thing, and fortunately what students ask from us is not beyond our power to provide. "If you don't respect us, we won't collaborate with you" is a message with far deeper meaning than we often give it. It can sound merely sassy, or it can help us reach deeply into what we all require in order to feel members of a community. Are students citizens, this book asks, or subjects? Once we ask this, we must also wonder about how others in our schools see themselves. They too need membership, if they are to reach out respectfully to the young.

If we want schools to pass on the highest values of our society, we should design them around those values. Then, kids would experience the school as an introduction into a profoundly respectful community of co-learners, co-investigators, in which they may be novices but not inferiors.

Every page of this book speaks to these issues, asking us to reinvent the settings in which we intend to raise our young. We need to rethink the time available for families to connect with their children. We need to design neighborhoods that support such intergenerational inclusion. And certainly, we must reconceive the schools, which we fund for just this purpose.

In all the current wave of reform, it's amazing how little anyone asks us to listen to the voices of students. Young people rarely make an appearance on the stage of this current conversation around "upping the standards," competing better in the world of commerce, meeting the needs of colleges and employers, and on and on.

None of that conversation will amount to much if we have no loftier purposes in mind, and if our purposes do not engage the students of our schools. Young people may at first look suspiciously at our intrusion, even resist it. But what Kathleen Cushman reminds us is that they are asking for us to enter their world, and to join ours as well. Until we make it one world, across generations, our lofty ends are unreachable.

Preface

THIS BOOK EMERGED AS A SEQUEL TO *Fires in the Bathroom: Advice for Teachers from High School Students*, in which students speak about teaching and learning in the classroom. When teachers around the country responded with great interest to its 2003 publication, MetLife Foundation, which had suggested and sponsored its research, saw an opportunity to extend the conversation even further. MetLife Foundation's commitment to furthering strong partnerships between young people and adults gave rise to its support of the research for *Sent to the Principal*, helping students raise their voices on issues of school culture that typically depend more on the principal's attitudes and actions than on those of teachers. In 2003, MetLife's national survey of teachers, administrators, parents, and students had also revealed a significant gap between how principals viewed their leadership and how teachers and parents experienced it.

To find students to contribute to the book, we sought a range of youth, some with leadership experience and some without it. In Boston, Massachusetts, we worked with members of the district's Student Advisory Council; for facilitating that connection we owe thanks to Keith Love and Barbara Locurto from the district and to Jenny Sazama and Rachel Gunther at Youth on Board. In Oakland, California, Michele Levine heads the district's youth leadership effort; she welcomed us into its work and arranged individual conversations with students. Darrick Smith at Oakland Technical High School gave us access to the students in his extraordinary leadership classes there. In Houston, the A+ Annenberg Challenge helped us work with students from schools large and small, urban and suburban. In Napa Valley, California, Nelson Russell brought together several students from the continuation school in which he teaches; in New York City, Martin Davis arranged several more from the high school where he is a parent leader. The generosity of all these people and organizations in finding time and quiet settings for our work with students contributed enormously to its candor and depth.

In addition, we called on conversations with students who had contributed to past research in which we have sought their ideas on making high schools better. Some students quoted here worked with What Kids Can Do on its Students as Allies initiative, for example; some participated in a documentation project at High Tech High in San Diego, California.

Once transcribed and organized, we showed the words of students to three seasoned public school principals, asking them how young people's hopes might fit into the workaday perspective of a high school leader. After talking with them at length, we added to the book their descriptions of experiences from their own practices that lent perspective and wisdom to the issues students raised. For these contributions, we thank Olivia Ifill-Lynch, a longtime school administrator in New York City who is now at the School Redesign Network at Stanford University; Lynn Haines-Dodd, the principal of McClymonds High School in Oakland, California; and Teri Schrader, who leads the Francis W. Parker School in Devens, Massachusetts. Special thanks go to Teri Schrader, who worked with us on chapter-end "homework for principals" exercises that administrators might use one their own or with colleagues.

The book could not have come together without Montana Miller's exacting rendition of hours of taped conversations, along with her extensive research assistance and perceptive ethnographic advice. In organizing the material, Barbara Cervone and Celia Bohannon contributed critical support, and Eliza Miller advised on matters of tone. In its end stages, the manuscript benefited greatly from Lisa Rowley's major reorganization and meticulous copyediting.

The real stars of *Sent to the Principal*, of course, are its student contributors, who spent many hours thinking through the dilemmas of school leadership and the nuances of school culture. As one student told us, "You really have to be a brave seventeen- or eighteen-year-old to go against all these adults, especially when they can pull the experience card. They're much older than us, and they assume that they know more." From our hearts we thank them for that bravery, hoping that they will keep on thinking and talking about these things in the many years of change that lie ahead.

KATHLEEN CUSHMAN
Harvard, Massachusetts
March 2005

Introduction

On an otherwise normal school day in the winter of 2004, the principal of a well-regarded big city high school walked out of his office during lunch period to find hundreds of students sitting on the floors of the halls in an act of protest.

About twenty percent of the school's three thousand students, upset that he had closed off the hallway areas where they hung out and socialized during their free periods, had organized in defiance.

The scene was a principal's nightmare. Mr. Randolph (let us call him) knew the power of his office; he could summon security guards, identify all the students participating, and mete out consequences for their disruption. But he could not erase the dramatic image before him. And he knew that this moment had just taken root in the school's institutional memory, as well, to grow larger and more vivid every time students retold it.

An experienced principal, Mr. Randolph spent much of his professional life trying to keep order in his school. He had plenty of good reasons for his earlier decision about the hallways, and he knew that he could deal with this day's crisis. But as he faced the mass of kids in the halls that day, he realized that students had their own culture in his high school, and he was a stranger to it.

Very few of the students who worked on this book have ever sat down in the hallways to express their alienation from the way their high school works. More often, kids take a more indirect form of resistance. They come in late or ditch their classes. They act up in class or simply sit through it passively, passing notes. One or two might write critical editorials in the school paper; lots more scrawl graffiti on the walls. Some start fights or set fires in the bathroom wastebaskets.

But all these actions have one thing in common with Mr. Randolph's sit-in. They are messages, sent to the principal by high school students. And if you know how to read them—which this book aims to help you do—those messages contain the crucial ingredients of school success.

In the current climate of school improvement, no one feels more pressure than a high school principal. If you head up a high school—whether large or small, urban or suburban or rural—you bear responsibility not just for the organization's daily functioning but for the performance of its students in high school and beyond. You hire and supervise teachers. You set expectations and consequences for behavior. You manage the budget and oversee the physical facility. You advocate for policies and reach out to the community. In the eyes of students, teachers, parents, taxpayers, even state officials, you stand for the school. You own its successes and its failures.

That is one way of thinking about high school leadership, and from it result many admirable deeds. You might, for example, follow the far-reaching recommendations of the National Association of Secondary School Principals, in its 2004 publication *Breaking Ranks II: Strategies for Leading High School Reform*. By making innovative changes in your high school's design—such as breaking schools into smaller units, creating personal learning plans, or grouping students in more flexible or equitable ways—you may already be taking important steps toward transforming your high school into a real learning community.

The students who helped write this book, however, do not think of school in terms of its design. They come to school because they have to. They come to see their friends. They know they had better come if they want to do well in life. And if at school they find adults who acknowledge them as interesting people and help them try new things, they also come to work side by side with you and to learn the habits they will live by.

The sit-in at Mr. Randolph's high school felt different to many students than it did to him, according to Eleonora, a petite eleventh-grader with long dark hair. Kids knew what consequences they might suffer for their protest, in a competitive academic high school where the principal's word could make or break their futures. In their view, the principal held the lion's share of the power.

> I was really afraid that we would get marked down for cutting classes, and my mother would be called. Students are really scared of the principal and the assistant principals. I feel like I'm powerless—there's the giant administration, and there's us. — ELEONORA

Eleonora remembers the reason Mr. Randolph shut down their right to hang out in the hallways; kids had been leaving trash in the areas, and teachers complained. She acknowledges that he had a point. But even though she serves in the student government, she says that she and her schoolmates do not have the kind of relationship with the principal that would allow them to work out a solution together.

> We don't feel like the administration would ever cooperate with us or find a common ground about a problem. Most of the time students won't approach the administration, and that's sad, it's really horrible. It's like living in a house where you can't approach your parents. — ELEONORA

Just like millions of other students in high schools around the country, Eleonora experiences her school as something done to her, not something she herself might help to shape. Adit, whose dark Indian hair erupts in dyed red hues around his face, explains.

> A student walking into the high school sees the building and the administration, the principal and sometimes the faculty, as a separate entity that he is opposed to, not on the same track. But school shouldn't be like a brainwash camp, just a solid institution that the students butt their heads against. It's gotta be a dynamic entity that we have a vested interest in making better, and more enjoyable, and more profitable for us. – ADIT

As far as Mr. Randolph was concerned, kids who left trash in the hallways were signaling their lack of respect for the institution, and so closing off the hallways had a certain logic. But the students took another meaning from his action. To Alex, the student body president, it showed that the principal did not consider the institution *theirs.*

> They tried to section off certain areas where we can hang out and can't hang out, and we felt like our liberties were taken away, because this is our school. We should be able to go anywhere we want. – ALEX

If Mr. Randolph had thought of school in the way Adit described—as "a dynamic entity" that students have "a vested interest in making better, and more enjoyable, and more profitable for us"—he would have made the problem theirs to solve. Instead, it seemed to students like one more instance of the principal telling them what to do, one more indignity that held them powerless.

> The students' initial response to what the principal wants to do is "No," and the principal's initial response to what students want done is "No." It's an automatic reaction. The principal wants to put more restraints on the students, and the students want more freedom from the principal. Unfortunately the principal is on top and you're on the bottom. – ELEONORA

When the principal always wins that power struggle, teenagers take it as a very personal judgment about them. They may have reached physical maturity, they may drive cars, hold down jobs, help their families, and negotiate a complex and changing world—but they can't have a say in how their school works.

> If the administration insists on making and enforcing policies that show that they're aloof and they're in charge, and what they say goes, it devalues the student, and it kind of inflates the principal. – ADIT

Teenagers rarely stay passive in a situation like this. They are driven by a pressing developmental need to establish an identity, and they will seek out anyone that helps them find it. If their high school administration does not hear their voices, respect their perspectives, and use their energies, they will ally themselves with another group that does. And a profound gap may then open between the principal's high school and that of the kids—two cultures (or more) overlaid on each other, in an uneasy tension that invites continual resistance and repression.

⁓

But that does not have to happen, according to the students who helped write this book. Adit's comment, for example, suggests an approach that involves neither resistance nor repression. Instead, it regards students (just like adults) as active investors in their school. An investor puts something of value into an enterprise, and also expects to have a say in how it conducts its business. If all goes well, investors also realize a return on whatever they expend, further increasing its value and benefit to them.

We often think of adults as investing their time, effort, ideas, even money in making schools better. But if we took *students* equally seriously as investors, we all might realize far greater rewards: increased interest and motivation, better communication, a more welcoming working environment, and improved learning outcomes.

What can the principal do to reframe the culture of high school in such terms and begin to see such results? What might allow students to trust the invitation to join adults as investment partners in making schools better? The teenagers who worked on this book say that the answer does not lie in sweeping or dramatic changes. Instead, they speak of little things that make a big difference.

When Kevin stays late to use the school's computer, for instance, his principal sometimes offers him a ride home. Enka's principal noticed a summer program she might enjoy and pointed her toward it. Katie's put a few comfortable couches in student gathering spots. Danesia's got students to survey their peers on ways to make school better.

Each of these small things made students feel that they mattered. They probably wouldn't show up on anyone's list of leadership strategies, although they do align with best practices detailed in *Breaking Ranks* and elsewhere. They derive less from a checklist or strategy than from an attitude—and that attitude is contagious.

RaShawn, a lanky junior with corn-rowed hair, attends an urban high school long labeled "failing" by its district. He says that when school leaders show students that they respect their opinions in the little things, they send a message of confidence and high expectations that pays off in bigger things, too.

> When they give us more responsibility than they usually would—other people might call it challenging us—they show that they trust us to accomplish it. Giving us more say in our education means that they think we're capable. They trust us to make the right decisions about our learning, about our daily experiences at school. That would be a huge benefit to all the entire student body, rather than a liability for the administration. – RASHAWN

Little things can also make a big difference in a negative way, of course. Jose wishes the cafeteria would let him take the items he wants for lunch and leave the others behind, not issue lunch as a package deal. In Ernesto's school, the principal made an executive decision to throw away any hats students wore inside the building. In both cases, the boys felt alienated by the way adults had decided to impose order on the school. When Ernesto kept his hat pulled over his ears as he went to class one bitter winter morning, he says he knew it was against school policy.

> But who are you to throw away something that I bought? I don't have parents, but if I did, I would tell them to come in and talk to her, because I have to go to work today and I need my hat. I understand that I was wearing it, but that doesn't mean that she can throw it away in the garbage. She could hold it till the end of the day, then give it back. — ERNESTO

Ernesto's principal probably saw strict rule enforcement as necessary to learning, and she had a point. But a small act of empathy, instead of a small act of control, would have allowed Ernesto his dignity and respected his individual circumstances. It might have even made him an ally in maintaining fairness and order in the school.

Each small interaction between an adult and a high school student has enormous influence in shaping that adolescent's developing sense of self. And, like all of us, teenagers learn from making those relationships.

> You can't look down on someone as if they have a lesser intelligence. You've got to give them the opportunity to prove themselves, and give them the benefit of the doubt that they can improve themselves. At the same time, you have to really make them feel like you really care—not like you're just trying to control the situation. There's got to be some kind of emotion in it, that it's more than just a job. That means constant communication about expectations and about how people are doing—but encouragement at the same time. A principal needs to know what the student goes through, and what causes certain things like being late and absences. — RASHAWN

We saw this message play out powerfully in the first book we wrote with students, *Fires in the Bathroom: Advice for Teachers from High School Students.* In what they said about their classroom experience, its young co-authors gave vivid testimony about what helped motivate them, engage them, win their respect, and overcome the obstacles to their learning. And because students spend so many hours in classrooms with teachers, their experiences came alive with the often painful details of up-close observation.

But kids typically don't know as much about the principal as they do about their classroom teachers. If they see the principal at all, it is in passing moments, like a greeting in the hallway or at a basketball game, or in more formal settings without much interaction, like announcements over the intercom or talks before a school assembly. The exceptions generally are when students participate in student government or get into some kind of trouble. So we sought out students in both those situations to contribute to this book.

From student advisory councils and leadership classes, we recruited students who knew something of the pressures and problems a principal faces in leading a successful school. We also took kids who had sat in the line outside the principal's office awaiting some disciplinary action. But as these two kinds of students spoke, we found that they were saying virtually the same things.

They talked about lunch and dress codes and student parking. They spoke of hall passes, detention, vending machines, surveillance cameras. They described the principal who came to the dance and did the "funky chicken" and the one who walked to the subway with kids to make sure they got there safely. They talked about the principals who kept their doors open, knew their names, cared what went on in their lives. They told what made them drop out, and what made them want to come to school.

If students knew when they woke up in the morning that they were going to a school where their opinions affected how the school ran, how their teachers acted towards them, and that what they had to say really mattered in what changes were made in the school—they would really come. It wouldn't just be an education that processes them, but one that they could affect and shape to benefit the student body. – RASHAWN

It doesn't take a sit-in for kids to say what Mr. Randolph heard that day: "If you don't respect us, we won't collaborate with you." That message gets sent to the principal every day, in almost unnoticeable acts of resistance or disruption, apathy or alienation.

But when students sense that you do respect them—no matter how small the ways in which you show it—something starts to change in a high school. Everyone notices, from the newest ninth-grader to the highest state school officer. The difference, Adit says, is "to make people *care.*"

The kid is a thread and the school is like a fabric, and you want to weave that kid into the fabric. You want to make it so that he has a vested interest in the patterns that the fabric of the school makes. You don't want him to be like the piece of lint on the side. You need to weave the student into the dynamic of the school and make him interested in, make him respect, the workings of the school, rather than see it as just another opportunity to show his defiance. – ADIT

In a million little ways, your students are watching to see whether you regard them as citizens or as subjects. In a million little ways, they will invest in school, if they see you as a partner.

CHAPTER ONE

Do you believe we can succeed?

To Danesia, the donut shop across the street from her big urban high school stands for everything adults expect from her—and what they don't. It's the place that most kids go when they cut class, walking out the school doors without anybody caring that they are gone.

But somebody ought to care, Danesia thinks. "My school has a large dropout rate, and one of the biggest reasons isn't academic," she says. "It's because kids don't feel part of the school as a whole. We all get sorted. The kids who are going to college go to one class, the kids who aren't go to tech classes, and the kids who don't belong anywhere get pushed aside. We were meant to walk out of school; we were meant to go to the donut shop. We were meant to struggle."

LIKE DANESIA, MOST HIGH SCHOOL STUDENTS pick right up on what they are "meant" to do with their lives.

If they come from privileged backgrounds, everywhere they turn they feel pressure to line up the courses, test scores, activities, and connections that will lead them to college and a rewarding career. If they live in poverty, a better future depends on some adult at school believing in their potential and caring enough to provide the supports to help them fulfill it.

Many of the students who worked on this book saw the principal as that person—the one who knew their names, showed them they mattered, listened to their opinions, and urged them on to success.

> My principal acknowledges every single student in the school. There's not a student that he doesn't know or care for. I don't know why, but he always notices me for little stuff that I do. — ASIYA

> He takes time to talk to you and ask you how you're doing, like not only in school but at home. — KARINA

Some principals convey that confidence in students by standing at the door of the school each morning, greeting them with a smile or a warm comment. Others regularly assemble student groups to talk about what they need and then take action on what they hear. Some hold drop-in weekly office hours; some lead a class or an advisory group. The best simply make a point of being wherever the students are, with their eyes open. They don't just notice the students who already excel; they see those who need extra support and take all possible steps to provide it. And students respond.

> A school worth going to makes you feel like you have a name and aren't just a number. It helps each student feel equal to another. — TRACY

All young people want to succeed in life, and they realize that what they do in school will matter. But many of their schools lack the conditions—both tangible and intangible—that help make success possible. Teenagers want to help change that, but first they need adult partners who believe in them. The best school leaders, this book's student contributors said, show confidence in young people's potential in these ways:

- **Know us and care about us**
- **Encourage us to take challenging courses**
- **Give us the support we need**
- **Mix us in diverse groups for learning**
- **Don't give up on us academically**
- **Show the community that you're proud of us**

WE CAN TELL WHEN YOU CARE

From the moment they walk into school, teenagers pick up signals about whether the principal believes they are interesting, likable people, each one an individual.

> My first impression was that he was a good principal, because the first day he already knew half of the people in the school's names, and in the hallways he would joke around with you. I think that's pretty nice. Some principals just go by you and act like you don't exist. – KARINA

> The first day of school we didn't have classes, we went to the cafeteria and got to know the students. He came downstairs, he was talking to all the students, like going around and trying to say their names. He was asking the freshmen if they liked the school and stuff, and he cared. – ENKA

Your smile, greeting, interested question, and genuine response all show that you regard each student as someone worth knowing.

> She was in her office setting up her paperwork, and she was nice, like, "Hi, I'm the principal and what's your name?" She got to know me, in those couple of minutes. It makes me feel comfortable, just to know that they have a different stature than just being some adult that punishes you. – KATHERINE

Students appreciate when the principal's relationship with them consists of more than just wielding authority. That can also lay the groundwork for resolving your future differences in an atmosphere of mutual respect.

> It's not always "school-school-school, we have to be strict"—they can also talk to you on a personal level, and they're human too, they like to do things. Like there was a parent dance, and one of the things was, "See [the principal] dance the funky chicken!" What? Our principal dances? Okay! – OSCAR

> If there's a new principal coming in, then that principal should not come
> on too strong, making up rules like you can't wear this, you can't wear that,
> you have to have a see-through book bag. Students will immediately rebel,
> cause it's like taking away their individuality. — APOCALIPSIS

By finding out what is going on with them, both in class and out, you show
students that you believe they can succeed, no matter what their situation.

> My principal knows most of the students very well, what we try to do at
> school and what we don't. If there's something wrong, like if you're sad,
> he knows, and he's there if you want to talk to him. There's a summer
> program I want to go to, and the principal tries to help, he gets your grades
> for you, whatever you need. He really cares. — ENKa

> Students have to know who you are, to trust that you are part of all the
> different cultures in the school. You don't only have Latinos, you don't only
> have Asians, blacks, or something, right? Go to classes, get to know all
> the different students, talk with them, get to know who they are, sit with
> them so they know who you are. Don't just sit in the corner of the class
> and look at the students; actually participate in the work, sit next to them,
> and help them out in the work. — LETICIA

No matter how small your gesture of support, it sends the message that you care.

> If your parents are not there, my principal almost like takes their place.
> He's mad cool, like he'll buy you lunch and everything. At our school we
> got laptops, and me and my best friend stay late in the office and work on
> our laptops, whatever, do homework. And every single day he brings me
> and my friend to our homes, he drops us off, because we ask him. And
> when we're in programs that require a lot of money, he pays for everybody
> to go there. Everybody. — KEVIN

Our school has all these programs, for example "Sister to Sister" for the females, and we're able to release our stress and talk about what's going on. And the principal drops in every now and then, and if there's anything going wrong in our house, then our principal will be there for us.

— APOCALIPSIS

HOW FAR DO YOU THINK CAN WE GO?

The adults in a school set an important tone when they convey a belief that every student can succeed. They don't play favorites—with high-achievers, with star athletes, or with particular ethnic groups.

> In middle school I had a principal who wanted all the Latin females to push forward in their lives and be the best. She would basically recognize them more, and I didn't feel that she really cared about all the other cultures. I understand that she wants the females from their culture to pull out, but you got to treat everyone equally, 'cause they're still your students, and all of them matter. — APOCALIPSIS

> As a principal you need to be able to unite all the different groups. Get everybody together, not just little separate groups. Try to see their families.
> — LETICIA

Teenagers tune in to the ways that adults treat them differently depending on what they expect of them. If you only let certain students take challenging courses, the others quickly figure out that you consider them unworthy.

> I wanted to take honors Algebra 2, and they told me it didn't have enough space. I was mad, I didn't think that was fair. I got As all throughout math last year. — BOHB

It feels condescending to kids when you do not encourage them to stretch academically.

My brother wants to get pre-AP geometry, and they're not letting him take it because they say that they want him to look good—they don't want him to stress out on it, they don't want him to get bad grades, because right now he's like an A student in algebra. – ELOY

But when you push them to do their best, students try hard to live up to the high expectations. And a little public recognition goes a long way.

Whenever there's good news, our principal always acknowledges it. When we got into [the city's student council], she went up to our teachers and told them, and she announced it in the school. We could go up to her and tell her anything. Like if we have a new baby brother, she'll be like, "Oh, congratulations," and just seem so happy for you. – KATHERINE

I'm a senior, and my principal came to me and asked me what schools I applied to, what schools I got into, and she makes sure that whenever anybody gets an award or anything, it gets posted in the bulletin. You know, she's so happy for you, she'll give you a hug. – TAINISEL

A SUPPORTIVE ARM AROUND

Students are more likely to get the kind of encouragement they need when every student has an advocate or adviser, someone who knows them well and can help set goals and keep track of progress.

Students need extra attention. A guidance counselor has so many issues and students to deal with, you have to try a number of times to set up an appointment, and it's just too hard. Even then, they really won't give you that much attention; basically you do get ignored. Maybe the teachers could take on another role as the advisor. – OSCAR

Without such an adult on their side, kids without clear goals can end up taking the path of least resistance. For example, when Tisha's large high school divided into academies with themes like leadership, technology, and the arts, she noticed the lack of personal attention to students' choices.

> Some students would be, like, "I'm not a leader, I'm not good with computers, so I'll go to the arts academy so I can just draw for the whole year." And that's not really good for the student. You have to dig deep into what a student really wants, because some students will be, like, "I'll just go for an easy grade." — TISHA

In such cases, those with the most savvy and persistent parents are likely to win out.

> I was in pre-AP courses, and this guy wanted to be in them, too, so his mom came up to school and got him into my classes. But when he came in they had to kick a girl out, and she was forced back down into regular classes. She's not a fighter, and her mom doesn't speak English that well, so even if she told her, her mom probably couldn't do that much. I thought that was wrong. — IAN

Students need advisers for more than academic reasons. Personal struggles can affect their success, too, and an adult who notices them can make a big difference.

> Some students, they don't have anybody to talk to, and they take all those thoughts and feelings they have, they hold it inside, and all of a sudden they explode with anger because they don't have anybody to talk to. They have academic counselors, but someone who has like a psychology major, someone with the human sciences, could really help. — TISHA

> My school is divided into three houses, and the house coordinators and advisors are always with the students. So if there's anything that goes wrong, they always know what's happening. Every morning when I look for

my advisor, she's in the office with other advisors or talking to the principals and telling them what happened the day before, and what they're setting up, and if a student has a problem, or whatever. — KATHERINE

SOME WAYS TO GET TO KNOW STUDENTS BETTER

- Set up advisory groups, in which up to fifteen students meet regularly with a teacher who serves as their coach, adviser, and advocate in both personal and academic matters.

- Ask teachers to pass out questionnaires at the beginning of a course, asking about students' interests, concerns, expertise, and life outside school.

- Organize events at which students can share their interests or expertise with an audience of peers and adults.

- Keep regular "drop-in hours" when the principal's door is always open to students.

- Have monthly grade-level meetings where students can talk about issues with the principal.

- Walk the halls and visit other places where students gather, asking how things are going.

WE LEARN FROM EACH OTHER

Schools convey all kinds of messages about their expectations of students by how they group kids together in classes—and teenagers are particularly sensitive to those signals. Some students say they do their best work in mixed classes that mingle students with various strengths, backgrounds, and academic records.

> If the only expert in a class is the teacher, the process of finishing a project is kind of slow, compared to if a group of experts teaches the beginners how to do something efficiently. Like if this group knows how to do Flash and other group doesn't, then if this group teaches the other group they both learn how to collaborate with each other, and they also learn Flash.
> — THAI

> It's different working with another person. You might have one idea of how you want it to turn out, but they have a different brain and they might have another idea. Part of the reason they have us do group work, I think, is so that we can learn to work with people we probably wouldn't otherwise want to work with. In college and in your career you might need that. Your boss might need you to do something, or you might have a team project, and you might have a co-worker you don't like that you need to work with to get the job done. — MAX

Mixing the high achievers with the low achievers may seem like a controversial move to many principals, but it can have a strong positive effect on the social and academic climate of a school.

> It creates a better environment. In most schools, people are just caring about their grades. It's like "Forget about you, why should I teach you?" Most high schools are about individuals, and at our school we try to be a community helping each other. — THAI

> You can't separate students and expect us to get along. You have to get us together, have us sit in the same classes. Put all the different cultures into one group, have them work together. — LETICIA

Making classrooms more heterogeneous does put new demands on school leaders. For example, teachers will need coaching in how to bring a group together in tasks that involve high-level thinking, at the same time that they provide the necessary instruction to students at varying skill levels. By making supports available to help the faculty manage that challenge, you signal that your school expects students to learn from each other.

> In some classes, if a teacher says "Pick your groups," the students will divide each other—all the Latinos move to one table, the African-Americans move to another, the Asians to another. They're going to go to their friends. The principal should say, "You know what, you're the teacher. You set them up in their groups, you pick them." — LETICIA

> The teacher could teach us, according to their class, about collaboration and the knowledge of each other's cultures. For example, I learned in history that the Africans would come to Mexico and teach them how to make pyramids. If they could work together back then, why shouldn't we work together now? — TISHA

DON'T GIVE UP ON US

High school students are well aware that some schools offer their students far more opportunities to learn than do others. They know they need academic support to bring them, step by step, to the point where everyone succeeds, not just those with all the advantages.

> Too many students are really unprepared for SATs and college. For example, our school is really poor, and other schools offer free SAT prep classes just

like a class. I went to my counselor, and I wanted to know about how I could improve my SAT scores, and he told me that I had to pay $80 just to raise a score on a test I know I'm going to fail. I'm poor, I'm struggling enough as it is. Why is it that you pay for college applications, you pay for the SAT registrations, and now you've got to pay for preparatory? – TISHA

Young people feel a fierce sense of pride and dignity, so how you approach their academic struggles is especially important.

I know people who should be juniors and they're still freshmen. Year in and year out, they just don't pass freshman year. How is it possible for them to be held back so many times? It's not fair; someone has to step in and make sure that they pass. Otherwise they're not going to graduate until they're like twenty-one, or even older! – KYLIE

Every little signal they get matters. After they stumble, they can either give up or keep trying, depending on whether adults respect their capacity to think, learn, and make better choices. They will respond best when you do not disparage their circumstances, but rather identify and build on their strengths.

When I got here I wasn't very good at writing, and I couldn't really get my parents to read my papers—they couldn't find the grammar, and we mainly speak Spanish at home. So [my teacher] sat with me after school, and she would have me read my whole paper to her. I caught things I couldn't catch at home. When you read it to someone else, you see all things that shouldn't be there. She taught me that, and now I'm a better writer—not up to the level I want to be, but I have improved a lot. – GINO

By contrast, punishing students for doing poorly can make them lose heart and give up.

When my older brother first got to high school, he was doing his work, but then he fell into the wrong crowd and he would stay up late at night. So at school he would be tired, and sometimes he would fall asleep. And instead of asking him what's wrong or what's going on, the teachers put him a grade down—he was a sophomore, and they put him back as a freshman. And that really got him mad. After that, he was trying for a little while, but he just got so aggravated, because it made no sense, they put him down in all the work that they were doing. He actually got sent to an alternative school, and that was being demoted again. The first day he got there he got jumped, and somebody hit him with a lock in his eye. So at the age of sixteen or seventeen he just decided to drop out completely. As he saw it, the system was putting him down, when he was trying to go up. – JOSE

Many schools provide a way for students to receive extra help. But everyone should regard it as an important asset, not a dumping ground for failing students.

I was in this accelerated academy where you could catch up on the credits that you missed from not making the right decisions in classes. But those teachers weren't taking the kids serious, and we end up being down there for longer than we're supposed to. So we presented that to the principal, because he was thinking about cutting it out, and he decided that we would have more teachers and tutors on hand. So now, this year, we have that, and I'm not even in the academy anymore, that's pretty cool. – JERRY

Academic struggles are not the only situation in which schools can send students the message that they are not expected to succeed. Suspension, though sometimes it seems like the only solution, has the drawback of removing the offending student from the community of learning.

If they know that our education is important to us, why do they threaten us by taking our learning time away from us? That's just keeping us from learning, keeping us from making our future better, and supposedly schools are made for the students' future. – JOSE

If you banish students to a different school, even as a last resort, you risk creating a class of outcasts with little hope for a better future.

> It's just like being sent to jail. It's just wrong. If you're being put as a bad person and you're really not, what's going to happen? It's just adding on to the fire. You get jumped, you get beat up, you get picked on. When you come back to your original school, all you feel is anger and hate towards whoever sent you there, because they put you in danger. – JOSE

> In order for some kids to get back on track they'll leave and go to a charter school, and they'll take extra courses to get ahead. But when they try to get back into the regular school, they take their credits away and make them take the class over again. At one school called CLC the teachers renamed it "Criminals' Last Chance." That's really, really harsh. – KAYLA

SHOW OTHERS THAT WE MATTER

You can powerfully boost your kids' confidence and achievement simply by bringing them to the attention of the community. When you connect high school students with outside adults, both sides learn how much they can contribute to the other. It strengthens not only the community's support for education but also the students' belief that their success matters to the world at large.

You might jump-start this dynamic by turning to the community for resources that students particularly need. (See the list on the next page for suggestions.) Once community members start to interact with your students, they are more likely to want to get involved.

> My school made a mandatory SAT test prep. You can take advantage of it junior year and get it out of the way, or you can take it senior year. You end up missing lunch and class, but you get help from tutors from colleges. And also they feed you; a local pizza place donates so much pizza! – JERRY

ASKING YOUR COMMUNITY FOR HELP

Schools hard pressed for funds can often find willing partners in the community to bring courses and services like these onto the campus:

- SAT tutoring
- Remedial tutoring in academic subjects
- Arts activities (dance, visual arts, drama, music)
- Service learning opportunities
- Career mentoring programs
- Student health services
- Child care programs
- Driver education
- Athletic coaching

Teenagers have much more interest in doing good work when they know that it matters to someone outside of school. In fact, few things have more impact than community connections in persuading high school students to persist in their studies.

> I've never really had much insight into where I want to be in the future. But I'm [doing community service] at a center for physically or mentally challenged people, and it's kind of broadened my horizons into what I might seek out. Working with these people, it just kind of really makes me feel good to help them out and to be friends with them. It made me think that this is the kind of career that I might want to volunteer in at least, or maybe if possible seek out as a full-time professional career. – BLAKE

> I'm a classroom assistant for a kindergarten class. We learn letters. They had to read these stories, and I went over certain words they had problems with. I don't know if it's helping me academically, but I think it's giving me a perspective on how I run my life later on—how I see other people, my position in the community. — MATTHEW

Students can gain motivation and confidence, as well as important skills, when you give them the chance to demonstrate their expertise before an interested audience.

> I was invited for a performance at the Hotel Intercontinental, and there was an open mike segment for any poetry that you had to say, spoken word or written poetry. Most of the poets were my age, so I thought to myself, look how many dedicate their time when they could be doing other things. I saw how emotional they all got with it; they were really into it. — JOSE

> I went with the principal to a convention, where 600 teachers from different states were talking about their teaching and students' perspectives. There were about fifteen students there, from nine schools. So every question they asked me was like putting me on the spot; I had to be prepared to respond. — THAI

They also benefit when teachers have them "show what they know" before an audience of peers or parents at the end of a course. One New York City principal makes a habit of sitting down with her faculty to compare the work students did for such public "exhibitions" with the results of their semester exams and standardized tests. "The exhibition represented what they actually knew and did," she said. "The tests showed only what teachers hoped they had 'covered.' It became a mutual conversation about what we know, what we want to know, and what there is to learn, for all of us."

Students themselves can come up with good ideas about how to make their work public. But they detest anything fake, so make sure you are celebrating their best, most rigorous work. Those who worked on this book offered some suggestions:

- A museum-type exhibition, either on the school grounds or at a public place in the community, like a bank, library, airport, hospital, museum, or convention center

- An oral presentation at a meeting of business people, civic leaders, parents, or educators

- A performance for younger students or peers at other schools

Don't forget to let the local media know whenever your students do something that merits public attention. It motivates kids to see their school in the news for something positive, just as it demoralizes them to see it run down in the press. Though they often know things are better than they seem to reporters and other outsiders, a little public affirmation can only help.

> When I first realized that I was going here, I cried, because everyone was telling me like, "Oh, they got riots, there's violence, there's racism." And I was like, "I'm not going to make it!" But then I came here and I saw all the smart people, all the good leaders that are coming from this school, and all the good people here, staff, students, you know. From what the newspapers say, they're classifying us as a poorer school, but I don't see that. They don't go look at all these honorable students who are trying to make a difference in their life, who really care about their education.
> — TISHA

Reading between the lines

Leaving school at 6:20 p.m. on a winter evening, you find Joe hanging out in the lobby listening to his Walkman.

You: What's up, Joe?

Joe: Not much.

You: What are doing still here? Time to be home, isn't it?

Joe: I had to stay to do my paper.

You: That's good! How're you getting home?

Joe: It's not done yet.

You: Are you going to be able to finish it tonight?

Joe: Maybe. [shrugs]

At face value, this conversation may have no hidden meanings. But every line of it could also contain clues about this student's needs. Add your own ideas to the following list of possibilities:

- Joe cares about doing well but needs extra time to do written work.
- Joe does not have a way to get home.
- Joe will fail this class if he doesn't do well on this paper.
- Joe does not have what he needs at home to finish his work.
- Joe has a job every evening from 7 to 10.
- Joe was kicked out of his house that morning.
- Joe is afraid to talk to the principal.
- Other _____

_____

_____

What can you do next, as Joe's principal?

You could say "Goodnight, Joe," and head home. Or you could take the conversation a few more steps to find out what Joe might need you to know.

What non-threatening questions could you could ask to invite Joe to share more information about himself with you? Write your ideas here:

_____

_____

_____

Once you know more about what's going on with Joe, you will be more able to support him. Choose any one of the possibilities from our list above. For the one you chose, answer these questions:

What can I do and say to support Joe in this moment?

_____

_____

_____

What can I do to support Joe tomorrow? Who else do I need to involve, and how?

_____

_____

_____

What can I do to support other students like Joe?

_____

_____

_____

CHAPTER TWO

Bring us to the table

As the end of school approaches every year, Katie and her fellow students sit down to fill out a questionnaire about their experiences at their suburban high school. Part multiple-choice and part open-ended, the survey asks detailed questions about the level of challenge in each of their classes, how well they feel known by their teachers, and to what extent the school climate feels safe, supportive, and inclusive.

Later, the school community—teachers and administrators, parents and community members, and students—gathers around tables to go over the results, and to create a plan for the coming year. "It's helped everyone to get a real full picture of what's going on," Katie says. "If I really have a problem, I don't feel like I'm just stuck. I actually have a voice in the school, and I can enjoy high school without feeling like cattle."

K ATIE SPEAKS FOR MANY HIGH SCHOOL STUDENTS who sometimes feel herded around by adults, with no say in the decisions that affect them. It doesn't seem to matter that they are at school to develop their critical thinking skills and plan for their futures. In practice, they must comply passively with a system designed by others—so it shouldn't surprise us when they look for ways to disrupt it.

Drawing young people into substantive conversations about school improvement, however, makes an almost immediate difference in the school climate.

> It makes me want to participate and follow the rules, because I know that even if I haven't helped create them, then the people before me helped create them. – KATIE

If school leaders make the effort to understand their points of view, students will reciprocate. But for students to know that their success is worth everybody's time and trouble, you must figure out ways to make two-way communication with students a regular habit.

> Students are the main source, and if you don't tap into it, then you're never going to know what to do. Every time something major is about to change about the way things are run in your school, like schedule or curriculum, you should run it by your students. And if it's something that would affect students in a bad way, and you can't do anything about it, then you should say that to them. You shouldn't just leave them hanging, thinking that you're the reason why their life is just going to be miserable for next year.
> — ASIYA

A principal in Oakland, California, at a high school that the state has labeled as "underperforming" after a decade of community decline, described how she followed Asiya's recommendation. She asked each grade in her school to choose two representatives and two alternates who would meet regularly with her to discuss matters of interest to students. She hoped for advisers beyond the usual high achievers or student council members, asking each grade to appoint "anyone they wanted, as long as they lived and breathed and came to school." She saw her advisers' role not just as planning dances and pep rallies but as raising their sights for the future.

The students' first session with her, over pizza and sodas, lasted hours. The group's members got to know each other and set some norms; they agreed, for example, to speak candidly but to keep private any sensitive conversations until they could report out together.

The principal bluntly told her young advisers that the city suffered from a shortage of qualified teachers. She would work on upgrading the current faculty's skills, but meanwhile, the leadership needed strategies to keep students on track to success. Together the group pored over charts showing student achievement and attendance broken down by grade, gender, and ethnicity. "Do you believe this shows something true about you?" she asked the students. "Do you believe that you can't pass a standardized exam—and if so, why?"

That began over a year of analysis and reflection, in which these students—once viewed as the problem, not the solution—began to act as co-investigators and planning partners with the principal. What would it take, they asked, to replace the current watered-down curriculum with more challenging courses for every student? Which teachers were proving most effective, when students contributed their best effort? What community partners did the school need in order to offer the enrichment that students wanted and needed?

Steadily, the word spread among students that the principal took their opinions and suggestions seriously. More students began joining leadership groups—some creating and administering surveys, some serving on the school site council, some involved in conflict resolution or justice committees. Although the student government still largely worked on dances and social activities, young people's voices began to permeate every aspect of the school, from the budget to buses.

That school still has a long way to go before its academic profile matches its goals. But everyone there—including the students—now expects it to happen.

The students who worked on this book offered these suggestions to principals who want to bring them to the decision-making table:

- **Consult us formally and informally**
- **Make leadership part of the curriculum**
- **Ask us to research student opinions**
- **Use us as ambassadors**

AN EAR TO THE GROUND

By staying aware of what students are thinking, both the positive and negative, school leaders create a culture that lends itself to collaboration, not conflict. Anything a principal can do to maintain informal communication with students will help promote the dialogue that prevents problems from escalating.

> We need to be aware of changes before. Don't let a plan be made just by adults. We need to know what's going to happen, to agree on what's going on. Let us help decide. Let us approve. – ZORANYI

> I can go to anyone, because the teachers and the principal, everyone in the school has so much contact with each other. You can just name people who feel the same way you do, and the principal will say, "Oh, I know them, I know what you're saying." – ASIYA

Holding open office hours is one good way for principals to hear what kids have to say.

> In the hallways you hear so many complaints about little things getting ignored. The principal should go to the students, maybe have office hours—something so we could actually talk about problems as opposed to just vent. – OSCAR

Open forums also help bring the issues out in the open, especially if the principal takes seriously the role of listener.

> We have town meeting twice a year, like an open forum by grade, it's about 100 people. We discuss things that have gone well, and things that we need to improve on, from the students' point of view, and then questions that they have. All of the administrators are there, and the principal gives us input. – TAINISEL

WHAT'S THE PROBLEM?

If you ask them, students can help think through some of the many obstacles to learning that exist in most high schools. They can do this in various settings (advisory groups, leadership classes, student government, school site councils) and on a range of topics like these:

- Student profanity
- Class disruptions
- Unproductive adult-student relationships
- Lack of study time in a supportive context
- Insufficient links with adult mentors from the community
- Inadequate access to health care or counseling
- English language learning problems
- Family or job responsibilities after school
- Money problems
- Lack of good food to eat during the school day
- School bathrooms in poor condition
- Size of the school (too large, too small)
- Too great a student load for teachers
- Overcrowded classes

BUILDING LEADERSHIP INTO SCHOOL TIME

Just as important as informal relationships are the formal structures that make student leadership central to the workings of the school.

Some principals involve students in faculty committees, as long as they do not involve confidential information.

> I work on a curriculum committee. Me and another student basically just go through and try to come up with things that can better the learning environment here and make the assignments more interesting. We go back and look at some of the old assignments and give suggestions. When we sit down in a meeting, [the teachers] explain what their assignment is going to be, and then they turn to us and they ask us what we think. We make suggestions like, "Well, that's not creative enough, and that's not allowing the student to show what they're capable of." I like it. You kind of get the teacher's point of view on the assignments. – JEREMY

Their comments about candidates for teaching jobs can prove helpful, especially if candidates are asked to teach a sample lesson, or if students know them from a previous school.

> Ideally I think the students should have a third of the say in hiring the teachers. A third should go to the administration, a third should go to the other teachers, and a third should go to the students. – ADIT

> The hiring committee actually talked to kids who had [one teacher applicant] as a middle school teacher, and the kids gave him a great reference. The committee didn't just bring in a group of friends that were in his class, they brought in different people from different class periods. – CRAIG

Kids know when their voices are merely tokens and when they really matter. Without good facilitation and a reasonable representation of young people, adults on school governance committees can easily dominate students.

The team was supposed to include the voice of students, but there were so many teachers that we were rarely heard. You would say something and they would notice it, but then they would say something else. – JANILL

It looks good on paper. But when it comes down to business, the respect is hardly ever there. The thing about the administration is that they feel that they are right. The principal doesn't have to listen to us. You have all the constituencies that make up a school, you have people who are elected, you delegate what should go to the parents, what should really lie in the students' hands. Everything should work out; however, it never does. We fight for what we really need, and things are settled for that meeting. Then at the next meeting it's brought up again! And we're like, "Hold on, we already voted on it, we decided upon this." Things like this happen. – ALEX

Class officers and the student council, of course, are the traditional ways that students take part in school governance. Bodies like these should not only function as organizers for social events, but as a pipeline through which kids can get their ideas to administrators on all kinds of matters that affect them.

Student government might be a popularity contest. It might just be who looks the best. But more often than not, we're also looking for those who can voice their own opinions, those who are loud, who can get attention, not only from the students but also from the administration. – ALEX

During lunch the student government has an open forum where students can come in and talk to us. Our executive committee, which is the president, the vice president, treasurer, and secretary, are on the school leadership team with the faculty, and we bring all the issues that we have. We can say we think this rule in the handbook should be changed, and then the principal sees if it's appropriate, and if she believes that it can be changed, we write a proposal to her. – TAINISEL

Every student, no matter how new to the school, deserves a voice.

> In my school, the ninth-graders don't have any student government.
> By not giving us that, they're saying that we don't have ideas, we don't
> have anything to say that would be important to anything or anybody in
> that school. – ASIYA

Many schools have elective classes in leadership, where students learn and practice important skills and take on adult responsibilities.

> We're like another kind of administration to the students, the liaison
> with students and teachers and administration. When there's an issue
> in the school—if the students say, "Oh, the bathrooms, we have no toilet
> paper"—leadership will try to tackle the issue by going to the people in
> higher power and say, "Okay, these are the problems, how can we deal
> with them?" – RAYNA

Schools can also use leadership classes as a place where students initiate and develop activities in which they have a special interest.

> I think leadership classes are the base of the school. I would hire a leader-
> ship advisor who specialized in working with youth and was very knowl-
> edgeable about how activities and events work in schools—homecomings,
> rallies during lunch, sports camps, non-academic things. – RAYNA

Sometimes leadership classes also motivate students to reach out to their peers on social or political issues, in school or out.

> Through peer education about problems in the world and about stuff that's
> real and that's happening, things like infringements on rights, we can teach
> a lot. A lot of adolescents have so much apathy, they're like, "Well, it doesn't
> directly affect me, so I don't care." Having someone who's your own age
> stand up there and talk about something means so much more. It leaves

people much more open for discussion, because they'll see their friend up there talking or someone they've seen in the hall. It's easier for people to open up in front of peers. — DEVIN

One of the things I've learned from leadership class is how to step up. I mean, if you see your friends doing some stupid stuff that you yourself used to do, you gotta be an example for them and say, "Come on, let's go to class, stop cutting, stop doing this, stop doing that!" If they still don't want to go to class, you be sure to go to class yourself, to move yourself forward. — DANESIA

TOOLS FOR CHANGE WE CAN LEARN TO USE

School leaders typically put a lot of work into the professional development of teachers. But often they forget to coach students in the tools that can help them make a real difference in their daily life.

With some training in survey techniques, focus group facilitation, or other fieldwork methods, for example, students can carry out important research about important issues in their own school. Their work may bring in even more accurate feedback than that gathered by administrators, because students feel more invested and more willing to speak candidly to their peers.

Lots of times students do not have a good relationship with the principals, vice principals, or teachers. But amongst your peers, you're comfortable, so you can talk to them about anything. Everyone in the school should have a voice about their school. — RAYNA

Helping students do research on the issues they care about strengthens the likelihood of constructive action. When students have all the information that adults have about an issue, they are far more likely to succeed in making a change. They can use their knowledge to sway the perspectives not only of their peers, but also of adults.

> Youth gotta be prepared to take the responsibility of making a change. It's not easy. You gotta stick to it. And oftentimes, as youth, we feel that we can't do it, so we just give up. Facts, you need facts. You need information. You need to be educated on what they're doing wrong. You can't just go up to somebody when you don't really know what you're talking about, because they can just run all over you. — DANESIA

If principals take their ideas seriously and give them opportunities to carry them through, students start to act more like allies than like adversaries. Several students who worked on this book, for example, conducted surveys of their schoolmates on academic pressure, cheating, school safety, race relations, and tensions between teachers and students. (See the Appendix to this book, "Students as Allies in Improving Their Schools.") Working with adult mentors, they analyzed the results, discussed them in workshops with staff and students, and presented them in a public "summit meeting."

> We made up the survey, and we got other students to take it online, and we gathered all the information up. It had to do with why people drop out, the wrong things that were in school and how we want to change them. We put them in hip-hop form, in poetry, and we presented the results to the students and at a program for the district. —JOSE

Almost immediately, they began to see results. One group of students wrote a successful grant proposal to renovate the school bathrooms, with the provision that students would participate in maintaining them. In another school, teachers listed all students' names on the wall of their faculty lounge, checking off those whom someone knew well to make sure no one was falling between the cracks.

Students know when someone is listening to what they think and say. When they can tell that adults respect them—including the styles, identities, and cultures that make them uniquely themselves—they are more ready to take up the challenges of school.

> The principal, as soon as he started seeing the aftereffects of what we were doing, performing and bringing out the statistics publicly, that's when he decided to start getting involved with us. That's what it took for him to actually listen to us. – JOSEPH

> If you feel it, then you're going to take part of it, and if you don't then you'll just sit back and let things happen. I don't want to do that, I want to be a part of it, cause I want to change the future for not only myself, my family. That's what's important to me. – VERONICA

PRACTICING DEMOCRACY

As students gain experience with working for change in their school, they begin to form the habits of democratic citizenship. Instead of just complaining, they act on what they see.

> What do you do when you're not happy with something in your school? First, I ponder it a lot. Usually it takes me a lot to think about what I'm going to do. I write a lot of stuff down, and then I talk to other students about it, to see how they feel. – ASIYA

> I wanted track so bad, and then I got a whole bunch of signatures on a petition and hey! Now we have a running team. It starts next year. I gave the petition to the gym teacher, and that was enough for him and he went to the principal. We have a lot of power. – APOCALIPSIS

> This year some students had problems with the electives, so we went and
> met with the principal. And he actually wrote a proposal and got money,
> so next year it will be better electives. Then we had about six meetings,
> we had a case study, and we voted for some electives that we'd like to have
> for next year. – JERRY

They know they won't get everything they propose, but as long as they can take part in the process, they are willing to compromise.

> I don't know how we pulled it off, but we wrote a proposal that we would
> be able to wear do-rags, hats, and bandanas. And we weren't able to get
> hats, but we were able to wear bandanas and do-rags for that entire year,
> just because we fought so hard to get it. – TAINISEL

Kids recognize that the principal must take ultimate responsibility for a decision. If you have already decided what decision to make, however, they strongly advise you not to put the question up for a student vote.

> A principal should never say that they're going to listen to the students
> and then not do it. If the students are going to vote yes, the principal needs
> to be able to accept that vote. If not, they should not even put that question,
> because then they'll lose complete credibility. Why would we ever listen
> again to anything you have to say, period? – OSCAR

Likewise, don't say something to appease students and then go off and take an action that contradicts it.

> My relationship with the principal demands that he'll be honest with me
> about what's going on in the school. That's a given, but I don't feel like
> I get it, and if I don't get it as a representative, I can only imagine what it's
> like for the rest of the students. – ELEONORA

If you are about to impose some new measure, such as surveillance cameras in the hallways, let students know about your decision beforehand. Better yet, consult with them before you decide.

> We had to arrange a meeting to figure out what was going on. The communication with them was horrible. It was up to us to come to them and say, "Hey, we noticed something in the ceiling." — ALEX

When you are open to the democratic process, students start to regard you as their partner in a mutual enterprise.

> When stuff actually follows through, when you see the change happen, you find a new respect for your principal that's been able to do that for you. We're not allowed to have a water bubbler in our dance studio because it's a fire hazard—entrance-wise, there's no space for it. One of the girls petitioned the principal to get a water vending machine, and now we have it. — TAINISEL

> The teachers and principals are not the only ones that make the school, the students also participate in making the decisions. If something is going on that we don't like, we have a voice to talk. They always hear us and try to make it better. — ISHMAEL

WE MAKE GOOD AMBASSADORS

Students know better than anyone else what their peers are saying about the policies and programs that you are deciding every day. You can take advantage of their expertise—first by asking their counsel on issues that affect students, and later by making them ambassadors for the decisions you have reached.

Older students also make valuable allies when you seek to help new students buy in to the values of the school. A cadre of "senators" from student government or leadership classes can visit home rooms, advisory groups, or class-rooms to initiate a conversation about matters large or small.

Students can also serve as key ambassadors in the larger community to which your school belongs. As a student leader in his innovative small high school, Thai often presents its philosophy at educational gatherings, and he has gained a great deal from the experience.

> It's very important for me to be prepared. Every word I say is having a great impact on the school. If they ask me something, I have to think carefully. I really care about representing the students here. Governors from different states come to our school to see how we are doing, because they want to create a school like that in their state. — THAI

Who's in the game?

For the fifth time in two weeks, the head of the phys ed program comes to you to complain that students using the gym during lunchtime continually leave lunch trash and muddy footprints and balls everywhere. It takes the fifth-period teacher the first ten minutes just to clean up so she can teach. "You've got to close the gym during lunch," says the department head. "Those kids will just wreck the place if we let them."

In this situation, what would you like your top three goals to be? Check them off on the list that follows, or write in your own goals:

☐ Appease the physical education teachers.

☐ Keep the school clean and orderly.

☐ Give students a stake in caring for the community's spaces.

☐ Help students and teachers learn to resolve conflicts with each other.

☐ Teach students that their actions have consequences.

☐ Other _____

_____

_____

What can you do next, as the principal?

Of course, you could just close the gym and announce your decision over the intercom tomorrow morning. But you could also decide to bring students into the conversation. That might take longer to resolve the situation, but it could also accomplish more of the goals you checked above.

What is one way you might involve at least some students in working out this conflict? Write your idea here:

_____

_____

_____

What do you hope this approach would accomplish?

_____

_____

_____

What worries do you have about taking this approach?

_____

_____

_____

Who might be able to help make this approach work?

_____

_____

_____

CHAPTER THREE

A place and time for us

After a rash of broken mirrors in the boys' bathrooms at one large urban school, the principal called student government leaders to his office. He couldn't put security guards in every restroom, he said, so he was going to lock up most of them until the problem was solved. "We understood his decision, I guess. We didn't want the school to have to spend all that money replacing mirrors," says Eleonora, the student body vice president. "But he wanted us to announce it to students over the public address system. We never should have done it, but we did. What were we going to do—he's the principal and he has all this power over our futures!"

In the next two weeks, "kids kept coming up to us furious, and it wasn't even our decision," she says. In a dramatic act of protest, one dissenter took it even further, secretly pouring bottles of urine in stairwells and corners all around the building. "It was disgusting for all of us, and really embarrassing for the school," says Eleonora. But she wonders whether it would have happened if the principal had looked into the bathroom mirrors and asked himself what students saw.

L OCKED AND GUARDED RESTROOMS are only one signal through which students get the message of "command and control" from their school's physical environment. However unintentionally, every decision you make about facilities, schedules, security procedures, and amenities conveys your philosophy about young people and their learning.

Do you run a place where authorities dispense information and young people comply? Or do you ask students to actively construct knowledge and to join you in addressing the difficult problems of living in community? Eleonora's story vividly shows that the answers can make the difference in creating a physical environment where students and adults can learn and thrive.

You signal that you care about students and their learning when your high school has attractive, well-maintained spaces in which they attend classes, gather in small or large groups, eat well, perform before audiences, and participate in physical activities. And you underline that concern when you involve them, and invest them, in keeping their school safe and welcoming.

> You've got to have an environment where the student actually wants to come. – LETICIA

> School should be a safe place to go, and kids should feel comfortable, have fun, and learn at the same time, not be scared and stay home. – SEYHA

A principal in a tough urban neighborhood might easily think that tight security measures like metal detectors will create an atmosphere of safety for students. But students say they dislike the presence of such devices, as they increase their sense of being prisoners kept locked up and under guard. For example, Seyha says he doesn't feel the need to escape from his new school, whose security measures are far less extreme than at his previous school.

> I came from a school where everything's strict, they have helicopters flying around, there's metal detectors to check your stuff, the fence is way high, and they're always patrolling around the campus. Then you come to a school like this where the fence is not even five feet high and the gate is always wide open. – SEYHA

Instead, students feel more secure in a school where adults know them personally and treat them as partners in keeping their workplace warm, welcoming, and peaceful.

> We used to have couches in the houses. Stuff like that made me feel like, "Okay, I'm glad to be going to this school." It would really help motivate me to follow the rules or make good grades. — KATIE

> It would be nice to have maybe a lounge for the students and teachers during lunch or after school or before school, just to sit and relax, with a little TV inside where they talk about political things. — MARVIN

Human connections like these happen more easily in smaller learning communities, which organize time and space so that students and adults can know and trust each other. But a host of other factors, from the buses to the lunch menu, play important parts in how students experience the physical surroundings of school—and either nurture or diminish the human connections so important to learning. The students who worked on this book described them this way:

- **Help us get to school safely**
- **Keep school on a human scale**
- **Leave us time to breathe**
- **We are what we eat**
- **Make security about relationships**

FIRST, WE'VE GOT TO GET THERE

Teenagers often navigate a rough neighborhood to get to the high school they attend. For many, the journey presents the biggest challenges of their day.

> Between the street and school is a mixture of negative and positive. Students are uncomfortable where schools are located, and it makes it hard to keep up our learning when you see the violence. We need more police

protection in our neighborhood, to keep schools from being mixed up with the streets. — ZORANYI

It's mostly the area that's bad, not the school. When I come on the bus it's eight o'clock and they're already on the corner, starting trouble. It's the early morning hustle—they don't even go to the school. In school you're being taught the right things, and then you go outside and see the wrong things. — JOSHUA

By staying alert to what students find difficult, you may find ways to ease their way and keep them safe. At the school Apocalipsis attends, staff members responded decisively when two students were jumped and beaten up in a near-by subway station.

Our school is [near a subway stop that] most students have to walk through, not a really safe area, and a couple of students were jumped and beat up. We had an assembly about it, so the principal could let us know a whole bunch of precautions—other routes, other options, don't walk by yourself, and things we could do to take care of ourselves. Also, they got more police in the area, and the teachers even went themselves, just to make sure students are doing okay. — APOCALIPSIS

Many teenagers avoid taking school buses, especially when the conditions of the ride make them uncomfortable.

I wouldn't mind riding the bus so much, if the bus drivers kept the people on the bus under control. A guy on my bus, he's running all over the place, mooning people, causing all sorts of problems, and the driver does nothing. And if it wasn't 100 degrees outside and we have to be on the bus for an hour. Buses with air conditioning should be a requirement for rides that last over a certain time. That kind of stuff is why people want to drive to school. — KATIE

But even access to a car does not make the journey trouble-free.

> We end up having to park on the street, and they call the wrecking company
> to come and tow our cars away. I don't think that's fair, because if the student
> parking lot was bigger and they didn't charge so much for it, we wouldn't
> have to park on the streets. – KAYLA

LOST IN THE SHUFFLE

Once they arrive on campus, many students, particularly those in very large
high schools, feel lost and anonymous. They shuttle through classes where
teachers have too great a load to know them well. And unless they get in trouble,
they have little to do with the principal or other administrators.

> My school should have signs everywhere. It's so big that people don't know
> where to go. – MEDINA

> The bell rings and people are gone in a flash. We have too many students
> and not enough time. The principal is always busy, the counselor is always
> busy. They say, "I can't fit you in my schedule, come tomorrow." We don't
> have them when we need them. That is a major problem. – ZORANYI

In smaller schools or learning communities, students may more easily form
partnerships with adults, in and out of the classroom.

> One principal has thousands of students in the school, it's too great a
> number for one person to handle. If every single one of us wanted to sit
> down with the top top guy, it wouldn't work out. You could take ten kids
> every day and you still wouldn't be done by the end of the school year.
> I think having small learning communities in a school is better. – JOSEPH

From the principal to the guidance counselor, adults can keep a more personal
eye on kids' progress and help steer them toward making their hopes a reality.

Now I am applying to college, and being from a small school I have almost too much attention! Not just for me, but for all students, they are asking, "Is your essay done? Are you sending out applications?" — ROSA

I wanted to become a teacher, but then I changed my mind and decided to become a vet. My teacher, who knows that, is helping me out and trying to get me an internship. At a bigger school they might not know you well enough to know that. — JANILL

SCHEDULES THAT WORK FOR KIDS

Teenagers' biological rhythms make them sleep later in the morning than adults and stay up later at night. High school schedules, however, rarely accommodate that need.

If my principal gave me an extra hour until school starts, I'd be there for the whole first period. — ASIYA

At eight, it's just like, "No, we don't want to come to school, it's too early!" Around nine, students are more ready to learn, we're actually there, our brain is there and everything. We're physically and mentally ready. So starting school a little later would definitely be helpful. — RAYNA

Once the school day begins, students say they often feel like cogs in the ever-turning wheel of high school routines. Serious learning takes time in which to focus and think, but the relentless pace of 43-minute classes creates considerable stress for both teachers and students. Kids in schools with longer class periods say that it helps.

I see a difference—we get the lesson done and get to the end with extra time. We focus more. Students learn more, because teachers have more time to explain the work. — LATISHA

But more time doesn't help unless the class helps students explore interesting things in a way that engages their minds and holds their attention.

> It isn't about time. You can give us all the time in the world, but we still won't learn physics if the teachers aren't good. – ALEX

Most students have little say in the scheduling of their day and little time to spend at their own discretion. Some take matters into their own hands, cutting class in favor of things they feel they need more.

> Sometimes things happen during the day and you feel sad or in a bad mood and maybe you need to talk to get something off your chest and you cut class. – TROY

An occasional stretch of less structured time would relieve the frantic pace and could give students the time to build stronger bonds among members of the school community.

> If the principal makes half days, like every two weeks, then kids don't have to skip school to have free time. – MEDINA

> It would be good if you could get a certain time during the school day, in a little class or different groups, and just get to know each other, just talk. You could communicate with every type of person, just not the people that you hang out with, whether they're gay or just a completely different style from you. – JOSE

With typically only a few minutes scheduled between classes, students caught up in the hallway rush often find themselves late to class through no fault of their own. Punishing them by lockouts, detention, or suspension can seem unfair, giving them even less chance to learn.

> If you give me more than four minutes to get from class A to class B, I might get there on time. – OSCAR

> We have tardy sweeps, where you have two times to be tardy and then you get suspended. It's not really fair, because lots of times students are trying to get to class; there's always reasons for tardiness. – RAYNA

> Our principal recently started to lock out the students. We have five minutes between classes, and as soon as the late bell comes on, he comes on the intercom, and he's like, I don't see any effort! He gets all loud, like, "I'll count to 30, you have 30 seconds to get to class!" And by 30 seconds the hallways are cleared out. If you get locked out, you have to go to the main office and get a detention slip, otherwise you can't get into class. – JOSEPH

It helps when teachers emphasize the importance of students arriving promptly and provide good reasons to do so. Rayna's science teachers, for example, start every class with a five-minute warm-up assignment.

> If you miss that, you miss points, and you can't make it up. That's a very good thing. It's affecting your grade, but it's more just a reason to get to class on time. – RAYNA

Rewards may work better than sanctions in motivating kids to get to class on time.

> We just come in and they sign a tardy sheet, and then our tardies decide if we can get early release, if we can go to lunch early, stuff like that. It really helps me. – KATIE

FOOD IS FOR THOUGHT

By his own description, Kevin is "a big dude," and to keep himself going in the middle of a school day, he likes a good plate of food. But a visit to his high school cafeteria just ruins his appetite, he says.

> They don't even have plates, they just throw little scoops of this and that
> onto the actual tray, like you're in kindergarten. The macaroni and cheese
> has hair in it, and the cheeseburgers don't even got any cheese. – KEVIN

Kevin eats snacks from the machine instead of lunch these days, but he thinks about food a lot. The ideal school of his daydreams, he says, "would have gourmet chefs, and that's it."

Gourmet chefs probably remain out of the question in public schools, unfortunately for Kevin. But, just like adults, kids look forward to lunchtime as a break from work and a time to relax, socialize, and restore their energy with good food. Not surprisingly, the quality and conditions of their lunch break prompt some of the strongest opinions teenagers express about school.

> I'm serious, if they want to survey us on something, they should have a
> survey at the beginning of the school year on what they should serve in the
> cafeteria! – KAYLA

> I think it shows respect to students if you offer us decent food and charge
> us fairly for it. I don't think even a possum would eat our school lunch,
> it's really very disgusting! It's disrespectful. – KYLIE

Many students have a growing awareness of health and nutrition and see their school lunch menus as particularly distasteful.

> I'm a vegetarian, and every single day I bring my two dollars and go into the
> lunch line thinking there might be something to eat. And there's nothing in
> there for me to eat at all. And I can't get anything healthy out of the vending
> machines. – KATIE

> It's supposed to be something nutritious, but I don't think French fries and
> chicken all the time is nutritious. – ELOY

They prefer to select items a la carte and object when the system forces them to accept food that will go to waste.

> Students know how much and what they're going to eat for lunch. They might give us like a chick filet and fries, and some pudding and an apple that are just going to be thrown away. They tell us to take it even if we don't want it. We either get those things or we get no lunch at all! –JOSE

With enough forethought about students' preferences, the lunchroom could match supply with demand and students say they would patronize it willingly.

> We have a horrible lunch menu, but there's like two items on it that are actually good. So when the good stuff is served, everyone gets in line, even people who normally don't even go close to the lunch line. If they come last, all the food is gone, so then they're stuck without anything to eat. – IAN

> If we had better food in the cafeteria, then maybe we would actually eat at school and not want to leave the school campus. –JOSEPH

But if off-campus lunch alternatives exist, older students especially want to have the choice to use them.

> Don't cut the off-campus lunch. That's the only true free time students can have to themselves. Keeping us locked up here will make school feel more like a jailhouse. – TROY

WE'RE PEOPLE, NOT PRISONERS

Lunch break is not the only situation in which students feel that school security measures—even those with the best intentions—can create a prison mentality.

Metal detectors, police officers, surveillance cameras, chain-link fences, and other tactics to control violence also feel dehumanizing.

> School can definitely get that prison feel. They're talking about closing campus, they want to put a fence around it and make it even more like a prison, and I guess beefing up security would also give you more of that militaristic vibe—people being scared, being shuffled from here to there. – LUKE

Students appreciate your concern for their safety. But they say that barriers are not the best way to keep people from doing harm.

> Metal detectors are a waste of time and money, because anyone still can come in here and do damage. Classrooms have paper cutters and scissors; you can do damage with a pen! It's weapons everywhere you go. – DEANDRE

> And if a student actually wanted to bring a weapon to school, a metal detector's not going to stop them. They could just drop the thing from the fence and go in through the front door, go back to the fence where they dropped it and pick it up. – LETICIA

They may feel that surveillance cameras intrude on the privacy of their social moments together.

> It's enough that we have security guards patrolling our school, but to have cameras watching everything we do—it's very demeaning. I mean, we talk to our friends, we have boyfriends. – ELEONORA

Kids realize that school security measures must strike a balance between effectiveness and respect for student privacy. But to achieve a climate in which students cooperate in keeping the school safe, they need you to treat them as partners.

School should not be a place where security is just like everywhere. Students should come to a school and not have to think twice about their safety.
—JAQUAN

If the principal starts bringing in things that make life impossible for s tudents, it's going to ruin our whole mood. We're not going to want to do anything. – LETICIA

If you must conduct security checks for the common good, students will submit to them with good grace. But courtesy, consistency, and common sense, as well as the law, should guide how searches are conducted.

When they're going through backpacks, they should do it like at the airports. You should be able to be there when they search your locker or any other stuff. I'd be mad if I came in and they were like going through my stuff. – MELISSA

Before they check our stuff, they should ask us if it's okay. They have to have a really good reason, like they saw you do something wrong; they can't just go in and start checking. Like cops on the street—if you're just walking around doing your own thing, they can't just pull you over and start checking you. – SEYHA

If someone within the school breaks the trust the community has established, students want the school to mete out appropriate consequences but not to abandon the offender altogether.

Any student that's caught with a weapon should be immediately removed [to] a rehabilitation program where they actually learn that they can solve these conflicts without trying to kill another student. – JAQUAN

But they resent when all kids have to pay for the misdeeds of a few.

The school locked up the bathroom, because the teacher found out some kids were doing drugs there. And so students aren't allowed to go during class periods, only during lunch or break. It's not right; sometimes, kids have to go to the bathroom. When the teacher says, "No, just sit down and wait," for me, I'm just going to walk out. – SEYHA

The attitude a school's security officers take can go a long way to establishing a tone of cooperation on a high school campus. Just as with teachers, students respond best to security people who set an example of competence, consistency, fairness, and respect.

A lot of security guards are lazy and overweight—they just yell. And sometimes yelling is not the key. – DEANDRE

They treat us like criminals. If you have a problem, they don't care, they won't answer you. They're really rude to us, it's just really upsetting. – KYLIE

Principals don't sit down with the cops and ask questions like, "What have you done, have you worked in a school before, do you get along with youth?" They just put them in the school and expect that the cop will do what he's supposed to do. I've seen in many cases a police officer disrespect a student, like if the student's joking around, he'll take out his stick and be like, "You want me to hit you across the head with this?" – JOSE

In the worst cases, students conclude that security officers have no interest in an orderly campus.

Most of the time, if there's a fight, they'll just be like, "Okay, let them fight, let them fight." They back off! Then if they see the principal coming then they go up and they're like, "Okay, break it up." – JOSE

It's like, "Go ahead and get it out of their system, so we can kick them off this campus." – KAYLA

At our school, they have cameras located everywhere, but nobody is ever there watching. – JOSEPH

Teenagers realize that they play a part in keeping their own school safe. But your part is making sure that adults establish authority based on partnership, not punishment.

We had a security officer last year who was an incredibly nice guy. He was really funny, and he actually got along with the students. And he made us not want to get caught by him. He was really social to students, but he was the kind of person who, if you did get caught doing something, then he would take you straight to the ground. – CRAIG

We're kids, and we're bound to mess up. Kids make mistakes, everybody's not perfect. We're not just doing it because we feel like it, you know what I'm saying? There has to be a deeper reason, a reaction, for every action. So don't just put us in a jail cell. We need—information at least. – KAYLA

Competing for space

More and more students are driving to school and you have a serious shortage of parking space for them. Only about half the students with cars have a place to park. Class officers from the junior and senior class ask you for a meeting in your office.

Senior: You've got to do something. Lots of kids are late because they have to park so far from school.

Junior: And if we park at a meter they're towing our cars. Plus a couple of kids got their cars broken into.

You: We only provide parking for teachers and visitors, you know. Whatever's left is all we have for you. That's just the way it is.

Senior: Well, can't you make it that only seniors can park there?

As principal, what do you hope for in this situation? Check any that apply.

- ☐ All students who need it have access to adequate parking.
- ☐ The limited parking you have is distributed among students fairly.
- ☐ Students and adults act as partners in resolving this situation.
- ☐ The situation gets resolved quickly, before it escalates.
- ☐ Other_____

_____

_____

What do you imagine happening if you responded in the following ways? Using your goals from the list above, write down your thoughts of how the situation might play out.

You say: "I'm sorry, but there's not much I can do about this. No matter what I do, there's going to be trouble with parking."

_____

_____

_____

You say: "We need to make parking a privilege you earn. I'm going to give parking spaces to seniors who have a B average or better."

_____

_____

_____

You say: "Why don't you pull together some kids and work out a proposal that you can bring to me?"

_____

_____

_____

You say: "Let's get together a meeting of everyone who drives and see what we can figure out."

_____

_____

_____

Do you have another way you would rather respond? Write it here, explaining why you think it would work better.

_____

_____

_____

CHAPTER FOUR

We can work it out

The day after her good friend died, Carly came to school despite her painful emotions. But she couldn't make herself go through the motions. Everything around her seemed empty and artificial, and when her feelings overwhelmed her, she made a defiant remark to a teacher and walked out of class. Catching her in the hallway, the principal met with only sullen silence and sent Carly back to class with a scolding.

"Emotion scares teachers and it scares the administration," Carly says. "Schools try to take emotion out of everything. But kids have to be there every day, and our emotions are just invariably going to conflict with our duties. They have to just accept that kids are going to feel bad. You can't punish us for it, and you can't expect us to just get over it, either."

E VEN THE MOST NORMAL OF TEENAGERS leads a turbulent inner life, filled with the anxieties that go along with any adolescence. When something further goes wrong—a friend lost, a family crisis, a bitter disappointment, a quarrel between rivals—kids often fail to keep their balance.

But, as Carly notes, they still have to go to school. As the place where they forge important relationships with friends and adults, high school often becomes teenagers' world, at least as important as home to them. Many kids keep going to school not for their classes, but because there they are figuring out crucial questions about identity. Will they become achievers, outcasts, provocateurs, peacemakers, or problem solvers? Every day may hold a new experiment designed to find that out.

The answers students arrive at will depend, in large part, on the climate of partnership you foster at your school. In every interaction, you can let students know whether they live in a world of tolerance and respect for individual growth and difference or one of humiliation and punitive control.

When kids get to school in the morning, for instance, do they enter a boot camp intended to keep them in line or an extended family of people who wish them well? Do adults spend more time breaking up fights or creating a culture in which people talk through their differences? Does it matter what's going on in a student's private life, or do you treat schoolwork as a completely separate sphere?

As principal, you have the chance to organize schoolwide routines and mechanisms that help teenagers feel supported as they confront the everyday challenges of acting responsibly in school. When they test the limits or break the norms, you can investigate what factors lie beneath their behavior.

> A lot of people do stuff out of anger, or because they feel that nobody cares. Sometimes, when people do destructive things, it's just because they need somebody to talk to, somebody that could give them advice. If everybody was assigned to a person that they could talk to and get comfortable with, I think it would really prevent some of that stuff from happening. Instead of kids getting mad at each other, they could probably find a way to solve the problem before it gets out of hand. — KAYLA

And when they make positive contributions, you can recognize and affirm them publicly.

> A student always wants to feel like they have accomplished something and they have done something positive. I think it's just how you approach the students, not making the student feel that they're always doing something wrong, but that they can do something right, and there's rewards out there for you to do something right. — RAYNA

Your interest, empathy, acceptance, and trust will not necessarily change the realities of growing up. But it can help teenagers find their way through hard times, becoming more confident and ready to learn.

> There was a lot of things happening, and I told my principal I needed somebody to talk to immediately. He doesn't make you wait a week, he does it the same day, even if he has something to do he puts it aside. And there's counselors in our schools, so I went to one, and now I feel better. — KARINA

The students who worked on this book had this to say about how adults could help create such a climate of tolerance and respect.

- **Show respect for our families and cultural backgrounds**
- **Treat our mistakes as learning opportunities**
- **Show us that you trust us**
- **Recognize that relationships are important to learning**
- **Help fairly resolve problems that come up among students**
- **Make discipline consistent**

WHERE WE'RE COMING FROM

Students often get important signals about where they stand in the world by the way their school treats their family. They quickly notice whether you give parents your respect or regard them as a nuisance or an obstacle. If they come from families without much education, money, or command of English, they keenly feel any differences in your attitude.

One New York City principal recalls a mother who burst into a classroom one day, demanding that her daughter come along to help her through a medical procedure. Called to the scene, the principal had to decide whether to support the disruptive parent or the student, who was deeply embarrassed in front of her peers.

In a respectful voice, the principal asked the mother to come to the office and sign her daughter out. Then she drew the student quietly into the hall. "I understand it's not fair to make you go right now," she said, "but you need to do it anyway. When you come in tomorrow, will you stop and let me know how everything's going?"

All parents care about their children, this principal recognizes, and school may afford the only arena in which they can make their voice heard. By listening well when they have something to say, she tries to send the message that the school welcomes and accepts families as they are, and shares their concern that things go well. If parents disagree with the school about something, she makes sure that students witness the respect she affords their opinions.

In all the routine business of school—parent conferences, notices sent home, community meetings, school assemblies—you can show sensitivity to the differences among families, and the possible difficulties they might have working with you.

> If you need to get information to a parent, you should be able to get it to them no matter what. You have a very high number of single-parent families, and you have parents who work more than one job, or work the night shift, so it's very hard for them to get involved. – JAQUAN

Students may feel reluctant to have teachers actually visit their homes, but you might arrange other ways for them to know better where kids are coming from.

> We had a [survey] question like, "Do you feel comfortable with your teacher coming to your house to talk to your parents?" And many kids said no. But [they agreed with] another question, "Do you feel comfortable with teachers going to your neighborhood to see how you live, what's your environment like?" – JOSEPH

If they know more about the family backgrounds of their students, teachers are less likely to tolerate the bias or stereotype that can sometimes creep into classroom discussions.

> Our geography teacher was talking about something she had seen on
> 60 Minutes, about a fanatical Mormon community out in the desert,
> and they're very extreme, and she's getting very personal, and I go, "Well,
> hey, my family's Mormon, and I know that not all Mormons are like that."
> So everyone's kind of looking at me like, "You Mormon freak! Oh my gosh,
> you have to get married by the time you're twelve?" – CARLY

And when problems come up with students' behavior or academic progress, familiarity with their families gives additional avenues to use in reaching out to them.

> Go and visit the homes of students who are doing poorly in class or have
> disciplinary problems, to inform the parents. – JAQUAN

GROWING TAKES PRACTICE

As everyone in the school community starts to know each other better, parents, students, teachers, and administrators all begin to feel more accountable to each other. Parents and students accept the principal's authority, but they also see that you respect their points of view. You recognize that adolescents need practice in developing good judgment, and so you treat their mistakes as a learning opportunity.

> As long as you show me that you respect me as a person, I too will respect
> you but not take advantage of you. If you are friendly with us, I can trust
> you enough and give you what you want. – MARVIN

Trusting kids to do their best rather than trying to control everything they do often brings better results. The more chances teenagers get to practice making good decisions, the less they will need to hide their actions from you.

> When administrators try to sneak up on us, we just know by the look in their eyes. They look at you strange, they're suspicious, and then we're just like, boom, we're not going to do anything stupid, we're just going to act normal. – SEYHA

Although at times kids will test the rules and push the limits, how adults respond demonstrates their belief that school exists for learning.

> Sometimes when you do stuff and they punish you for it, it makes the situation worse instead of better. We respected this principal, because he had a relationship with the kids. If we got in trouble, he didn't yell at us and tell us we were dumb. He asked us, "Okay what happened, why did you do this?" He tried to help us out and tell us, "Okay, I'll do this for you if you do this for me." He tried to make things better. [Otherwise] you're mad at them, and you're back trying to do something else to make them mad. – KAYLA

When your school assumes a basic trust among those in it, students begin to feel less like misbehaving children and more like valued members of a community. Older students, especially, often regard what may seem like small privileges—like the right to come and go from campus—as important symbols of trust.

> For the juniors and seniors we should get the privilege to go off campus for lunch and then come back and go to class. That treats us more like adults. – KAYLA

At Enka's school, the principal trusted students to show that they could have their music and still respect the classroom norms.

> Everybody wanted to listen to CD players with headphones, during break when we went from one class to another. The principal didn't really trust to make that a law, but they allowed it 'cause they were like, "We'll see what will happen." The students don't listen to it during class, they pause it but just leave it on their table, and the teachers don't mind 'cause they know it's turned off. And then during break they turn it on. – ENKA

Your positive attitude in coming to such agreements can make a huge difference to students, and give them one more reason to regard adults in the school as partners, not adversaries.

> We've been having problems with water balloons and water fights. So the principal said if we could go ten days without people throwing water bottles at each other, then we could have an organized water game on the football field. And that worked out—the hallway and everything stayed dry and we had an organized game on the football field, which was fun, and everyone got to participate. – RAYNA

> The littler things aren't so black and white. Like if the principal says "No knives," that's one thing, and if he says "No hats," that's another. Does wearing a hat in class really affect my math teacher's ability to teach? No! He has to give us enough respect for the little things like that. And that in turn will generate our respect for him and make us more likely to engage in dialogue. – ADIT

WE LEARN FROM RELATIONSHIPS

A trusting community grows more steadily if its members have settings in which they can get to know each other better. At their best, these types of get-togethers happen spontaneously, for no particular occasion.

> I have always wanted for kids to bring in their guitars or whatever instruments, and play at lunch. At my school we have that quite often, and someone kind of busts out into song at lunch, and it brings everyone together.
> — KYLIE

But you can also arrange informal gatherings in response to particular issues that affect school culture. When divisions developed among students at Ian's school, for instance, administrators arranged an ice cream social to bring kids together across groups.

> They picked out people that normally don't sit together and we had to sit down in groups of two and three and talk. They gave us ice cream and all the toppings, and there was this questionnaire to make sure you tried to learn about the person. It would have [been better] if it had been earlier in the year, but I think it really helped with mixing our school up. — IAN

By thinking in creative ways, a principal can also devise more formal structures that bring people together. For example, when new ninth-graders enter high school, strong and positive connections with others in the school may make all the difference to their adjustment. You might decide to group ninth-graders into a separate "house" for that transition year, to give them more support as they get used to the new demands of high school. But while this strategy may have much to recommend it, some students may experience it as isolating them from older ones who could help them.

> Freshmen coming into high school are nervous. It was like, I'm just now coming into high school, I have no idea what high school is, and they isolated us. So I cut class to kick it with the older kids, just to get a feel of what high school is supposed to be, and how students are, and how they interact. — TISHA

> The way the upperclassmen act is supposed to rub off on you, whether it
> be positive or negative—most of the time positive, because you want to
> be mature. If you don't get to interact with anyone older than you, it's just
> like another year of eighth grade. – JAQUAN

Many schools are also trying the advisory group approach, in which a dozen or more students meet regularly with a teacher who acts as their advocate in both social and academic arenas. Sometimes schools mix students of different ages in these "advisories," so new students can learn the ropes from older ones and watch their progress to graduation. Others group them by grade levels, so they can work through common developmental stages together. Some schools combine both strategies and pair up advisory groups of students at different stages, to create flexibility according to the need.

Advisories are an important way in which high schools can attend to students' emotional and social development. Academic progress may seem like the most important thing to adults, but students who feel overwhelmed by their feelings may find it impossible to concentrate on their studies.

> There's a lot of pain that just goes unnoticed. And when you have to come
> to school every day and you have to function, and you have to just bottle
> all this stuff up, at the end of the day you go home and you're just going
> to self-destruct. It's very hard, and I think every kid should have someone
> to talk to. – CARLY

If a crisis occurs in the larger school, the advisory group provides a safe place in which to help students deal with their emotions. Attending to their needs at times like this matters far more than trying to keep their minds on their schoolwork.

> In ninth grade I had a friend that committed suicide. And when the school
> found out about it, they refused to acknowledge it at all. When I first found

> out, my friend and I were crying, and my English teacher was just like, "You need to focus on school. You'll eventually get over your friend, but you'll always need your education." – KATIE

Sometimes the best thing a principal can do is to communicate understanding and sympathy at the unfairness and bitterness life can bring. You can't fix everything—and students do not expect you to—but they need to know you care.

> When my friend died from cancer, the principal called her friends up to the office, and he told us she just passed away. He told us, "If you like, you could call home, you could go home, or you could stay here. Whatever would do you better, just do it." – JOSE

WHEN WE DON'T GET ALONG

As they search for acceptance and identity, teenagers have an almost tribal tendency to group themselves in cliques based on social profiles, ethnicities, or various status markers. But you can help find ways to cross those divides, capitalizing on the adolescent passion for justice and fairness.

Kids look to adults to set a consistent example, in both attitude and behavior, that any put-downs are unacceptable. You can insist that every adult in school respond promptly to such situations.

> My school's mostly blacks and Hispanics, and this year for the first time a Hispanic girl came on announcements, talking about what is Cinco de Mayo. And the blacks were making unnecessary remarks like, "Why do we need to know this?" I'm pretty sure the teacher heard, but she didn't say nothing, and I felt that was disrespectful. – ELOY

> In middle school we had a Muslim girl who wore a chador to school every day, and in gym she wore a floor-length skirt. Students gave her a hard time, and she ended up leaving the school. I don't ever remember our

principal stepping in or saying anything. And you can't just have the principal tell the whole school, "All right, don't harass each other, that's it." The principal should tell teachers to be aware of what's going on in their classrooms and to stop harassment right when they see it happen. — CARLY

You only widen the gaps among different groups if you play favorites among students, however unconsciously. For example, kids will resent it if student council members are the only ones you ask to represent the school in the community, or if some kids get away with misbehavior because they have special status at the school.

The popular football players can start a riot or a food fight or whatever, they'll get sent to the principal's office or the cop's office, and they'll talk to them for a little while and send them back to class. But if a regular kid does it, they'd end up getting suspended, or something. After one game, the two teams got into a big old fight, and everybody got arrested except for the quarterback! And he started it! — KAYLA

They do whatever they have in their power to keep people that make the school popular and get the school known. If they send them out, then we're not going to win any more games, and they want our school's reputation to be good. — JOSE

Above all, students want you to react to behavior problems fairly and consistently. You can set a tone of safety at the same time that you respect the stake they have in the matter.

We need a principal that enforces rules and teachers that aren't afraid to approach students and keep them in line. That may seem like it's cracking down on individual liberties, but the reality is, if you have kids who are getting jumped and no one really feels safe, you have to put safety ahead of a vibe. — LUKE

Respect would help, some kind of dialogue between the students and the administration. But if you start "respecting" the things people do that aren't really legal or helpful to the learning environment, at some point that stops being respecting their actions and it turns into like, "They're faulty and they can't really deal with it so let's just let it go." But if you say, "Respect won't work, so we shouldn't even give them any," that's an even bigger fallacy. — ADIT

Despite adults' best efforts, conflicts among students are inevitable. When a fight does break out, students agree that both sides need time to cool down before they come together to talk out their differences. It helps to have the sense that someone understands what caused them to flare up.

Take them away from each other so they can calm down and breathe, because they're probably both really riled up. Then get both of their sides of what happened, and maybe some other people's opinions, and and talk about it for a while. — NICOLE

As far as keeping racial violence down, have teachers that are grounded with this one ethnic group talk to them, instead of the principal going in and saying, "Stop this violence or I'm going to suspend you." Students here tend to bond more with teachers that are from their ethnic group. It's different coming from a teacher who you know and trust. — JAQUAN

Nobody likes violent behavior, including students, and they do not want you to tolerate it. They appreciate your genuine concern for their safety, in a nation with easy access to weapons and an entertainment culture that glorifies mayhem. But they also recognize that tempers can flare, and they think school should play a role in calming them. To maintain a safe and peaceful environment, they say, you can do better than suspend the offenders.

What do you progress from that? The student hasn't learned anything, they just lost class time. Usually in high school, the fights that go on is really negligible. Like "Oh, she was looking at me like that," or "She took my man," or "I don't like him because he got my girl." It's not like a situation where you have to fight for your life. So instead of like, "Hey, you're fighting, I'm going to suspend you for two weeks," bring in the students and ask them one on one, "What happened, what was the fight?" – TISHA

We're still kids. We're influenced much more by peer pressure and by pop culture and factors like that. And it is up to the principal to be better than us, to respect our views and also to reach out to us. And be like, "Look, it's not cool to be a thug." Instead of saying, "If you're a thug you can't come into this building." – ADIT

They see injustice when a troubled student has no place to get help.

I have one friend that's been sent to long-term [suspension] three times. I mean, it hasn't changed anything! His behavior problem doesn't come from the school, it's something that goes a lot deeper than that, and long-term doesn't address the real problem. It's just an excuse to purge the "bad students" out of school. – KATIE

There's nothing constructive about kicking kids out of school. Or suspending kids, when in fact, you could have some kind of more helpful program for the kids themselves. In the end, you don't just want the safety of everyone. You want the kids to become better people. – ADIT

By coaching students themselves to resolve problems as they come up, you do far more than react to particular incidents. As you help them develop into leaders, kids step up to make school better for themselves.

Leadership classes are good, because they teach students that they do have this ability within to lead. It's just that some students may have to be trained a little more than others because they're not just naturally ready to lead. Students are taught through leading each other, from presentation skills to conflict management. That way, when problems occur, students don't necessarily look toward teachers or administrators, because they've been taught in the classroom setting that they can prevent these situations, and handle them, or de-escalate them back to a place where it's supposed to be. — JAQUAN

When leadership skills take their place in the regular curriculum, students practice new ways of looking at each other, and can gradually take a new stance toward their everyday interactions.

One of our first assignments, we had to go around the school using different words to talk to other students, uplifting words instead of words that put people down, and just see how they react. Like instead of saying the B word, you call somebody beautiful or something. The strange thing is, a lot of people reacted like you were weird, 'cause it's something they're just not used to hearing. You could just see how badly oppressed people are, when they get a compliment and they just don't accept it. — AMBROSE

Their insights and strategies for improving the school culture have all the more power because they come from the ranks of students, not from the adults in charge.

If everybody's fighting, there's probably a reason behind it. If you have tension all the time, let's say between the Latino and the black students, then it might be because they don't know each other's culture, they don't know each other. You can't separate the students and expect them to get along. You could have assemblies for different people at different times, but the most important thing is to have the students together. Have them united, have them collaborate with each other. — LETICIA

You would walk into the cafeteria and every race was sitting in their own tables. It's not just hate, you feel like those groups don't know you and don't want to know you, and so you tend to hate when you don't understand. You have to address hate as one big issue, and everyone has to talk about it. There has to be a balance of races in the school as well—you should deliberately mix classes, balance it out by ethnicity. That's unfair, yeah, but it doesn't give anyone any choice but to get along with other races and practice tolerance. And it leads to tolerance in society, if you've grown up knowing how to deal with other races. — CARLY

What's really going on?

You are passing through the cafeteria at lunchtime when you notice a small cluster around two big boys who have high social standing among the students. They have snatched the lunch bag of a younger, smaller boy and are hiding it behind their backs, tossing it over his head to one another, opening it and commenting on the contents. You approach the group.

You: What's going on, guys?

Big Boy 1 [casual, smiling]: Not much.

You: What's in the bag?

Big Boy 1: Sandwich, apple, cookies ...

Big Boy 2: Cheetos ...

You: Whose lunch?

Big Boy 1 [puts his arm around smaller boy]: Aw, it's his lunch. We
were just playing around.

You [looking at the smaller boy]: You okay?

Big Boy 1 [gives the lunch bag back to smaller boy, smiling]:
He's good. We're friends.

It's hard to know what's really going on when you walk in on this kind of situation. Sometimes what seems like harassment is really just horsing around. But if a student is feeling distress, you will want to do something to help.

As principal, what do you want to accomplish with your response?
Add your own ideas to the following list of possibilities:

- To maintain a friendly climate among your students.
- To keep the smaller boy safe from harassment.
- To help the bigger boys understand that they have gone too far.
- To show everyone present that the school does not tolerate harassment.

Other _____

_____

What might result if you responded in the following ways? Thinking about your goals from the list above, write down how the situation might play out.

You say, "That's good, then. Have a good lunch, guys."

_____

_____

You say, "Well, I'm not good with this. Give him back his lunch, and I don't want to see this kind of thing again."

_____

_____

You point to all three boys and say: "I want to see you in my office at the end of the day."

_____

_____

To the two big boys, you say: "I want to see you in my office at the end of the day." To the smaller boy, you say, "Can you bring your lunch and come to my office for a few minutes right now?"

_____

_____

Is there any information that could help you respond in the best way? Check all that apply, and add your own ideas:

☐ All three students' names
☐ What grades they are in
☐ What adults in the school know them well
☐ Whether this kind of thing has happened before with any of them
☐ Other_____

CHAPTER FIVE

We need to express ourselves

Jose comes alive through his music, dance, and poetry. He plays his guitar every chance he gets and has grown one fingernail extra long so he will never be without a pick. He commits his poems to memory, destroying the scraps of paper he wrote them on, so only he will decide who can hear them. He changes his appearance with his moods; one term he'll have spiky hair with dyed tips, the next he'll grow it long. And he loves to dance.

One day on a break out in the courtyard, Jose and a few friends began to dance, losing themselves in the motion and the music. Before he knew it, a teacher interrupted them, breaking up the group, and reporting the incident to school authorities. Jose ended up being sent home by the principal. "He felt it was gang-related," says Jose. As for him, he felt disrespected and violated, singled out for the way he expressed himself.

J OSE WANTS SCHOOL TO BE A PLACE where he can express his individuality in ways that matter to him. He's not out to deliberately provoke adults. But when he gets sent home from school for the way he dresses and dances, he grows frustrated.

> Hip-hop is like a culture for us, and we love to express it. There are a lot of adults, if they see something out of the ordinary they feel that it's gang-related. Like the lifting of the pant leg, one pant leg down and the other one folded up, up to your knee. Once that was gang-related, but now it's just the style. – JOSE

Jose has a point. Kids in suburban and rural settings, as well as cities, are wearing styles that originate in urban subcultures and gain national popularity via entertainment media. Some schools, especially those in areas where gangs pose a threat to student safety, address the clothing issue with uniforms or a strict dress code. But if teenagers can wear what they want, they will usually choose the fashions of the day—and consider it part of their identity.

Different controversies might come up when students express themselves in other ways. The football team, for instance, might spontaneously kneel down and pray to Jesus before the game, causing difficulty for students of different faiths. The marching band might wear political campaign buttons for an incumbent president during the homecoming parade, implying a school endorsement of that candidate. Maybe kids want to listen to their favorite music on headphones while they're doing silent work in class, but the teacher thinks it will distract them from their subject.

These are all complicated situations, and a principal could react to any of them by just calling a stop to it. But would that be the best response?

Most principals don't want to get bogged down in arguments about dress styles and music when the students are supposed to be reading *Macbeth* and solving quadratic equations. But what might seem like distractions from the work of school could well offer priceless opportunities for a school leader.

> So many problems could be resolved if the principals would actually sit down and say, you know, what are those about? Why are you wearing those? That would make such a big difference. – KATIE

Every encounter like Jose's between students and adults holds out a chance for learning—on both sides. Adults who listen well can learn from students about what they intend to say through their behavior, their dress, their music and art.

And as adults explain their points of view—rather than just imposing them—kids learn how to have a hard conversation about differing ideas and beliefs. Even if they still choose to push adults' buttons with their self-expressions, at least they will do so in an atmosphere of openness and communication, not on a battleground.

The students who worked on this book suggested these ways to show respect for the school's youth culture along with its adult culture:

- **Acknowledge our different perspective**
- **Give us a say in how we dress**
- **Recognize the importance of our artistic expressions**
- **Respect our right to speak out**

WHAT'S GOING TOO FAR?

Getting adults and kids to agree on what counts as legitimate self-expression and what falls into disruption or offensive behavior is one of a principal's more difficult tasks. The line is not always easy to draw, but deciding where it falls gives you plenty of chances to engage students and adults in research, hard thought, and stimulating discussions about things that matter to all of them.

For example, take a look at each behavior on the following list that students helped make, and think about whether it "goes too far" for you. Would you crack down on it, or would you consider it a legitimate expression of youth culture, identity, or expression? What factors would enter into your decision if you encountered it at your school?

- An editorial in the school newspaper criticizing the coach of the losing football team

- Graffiti written on the inside of restroom toilet stalls

- Listening to music on headphones during a writing period in class
- Wearing a shirt picturing a gun in a circle with a line drawn through it
- Wearing tight low-cut jeans with thong underwear showing
- Wearing cheap plastic bracelets that supposedly denote sexual experience

A principal's job is often complicated by the fact that just as students sometimes cross the line, so too do the actions that adults take in response. Like young people, adults don't always have the skills to communicate with people whose ideas or cultures differ from their own. That's where you can make a big difference when an issue of youth culture—whether it's body decoration, dance, or another form of self-expression—comes up against the conventions adults prefer to see in schools.

Students working on this book described an array of situations in which they felt teachers or principals had reacted unfairly to their behavior. And it's easy to see how the perspectives of youth might differ from that of adults about whether a particular behavior is "going too far."

You might think that the cheerleading team's choreography includes gestures that are too sexualized, while the motions might strike the cheerleaders as reflecting the latest dance moves. Or you might stop the members of a sports team from kneeling down to pray together before a game, when they think it will get them to victory. As every principal knows, situations like these arise regularly in the daily life of high school. But they can be learning experiences, not just confrontations. In fact, they involve questions so important that they sometimes reach the highest courts in the land.

How you involve students into conversation about such questions can help create mutual respect for the differences between your perspective and theirs.

For example, you could look together at whether the students' actions could be taken as an official representation of the school, which then might be liable for any negative consequences. You and the students might have different ideas about whether a certain behavior (either on their part or yours) disrupts learning, or creates a hostile or difficult environment.

You may also ask yourself whether repressing student expression might just cause more problems than allowing it.

> You cannot go on the intercom, just because you're the high authority, and just start saying everything that you want, you want this, you want that—it can't happen like that. You will have students rebelling against you, trust me on that. – MARVIN

It's pretty clear that no easy solutions exist to most of these dilemmas. Inevitably values do compete with each other—the value you put on an orderly school, for example, may compete with the value of student self-expression. But the very fact that you take the questions seriously gives teenagers the message that you respect their cultures, their identities, and their intelligence. That makes them more likely to respect the needs of the institution, too.

WE CARE WHAT WE WEAR

When teenagers dress for school, they are sending messages about their identity that matter enormously to them, but which adults may not completely understand. So it's no wonder that issues of dress so often come to the top of the list of things students and adults clash over. For that reason alone, it's a good arena in which to practice having conversations across the divide of youth and adult cultures.

The principal of a small public school in Massachusetts tells an instructive story about a school-wide conflict over the way students dressed.

A group of incensed teachers had come to her, proposing to institute a new dress code. Student clothing had crossed the line of decency, they said, to the point where teachers were embarrassed to look at a student—a situation, clearly, that interfered with doing their job.

But experience had taught this principal not to jump to immediate conclusions. Instead, she gathered the entire faculty to talk about what they saw students wearing, and how it made them feel in different cases. She knew they needed support, and sharing their discomfort was an important step toward that.

Then she asked the teachers to take up the subject with their students in advisory groups. Showing photographs of teenagers culled from magazines and family albums, they asked kids, "Judging from the clothing worn here, where is this person going?" The responses let adults and students alike gather important evidence about what kids regarded as the norms for clothing at school, social events, work, and relaxing at home or with friends.

Finally, in gender-separated groups, teachers asked students to talk about what they intended to convey when they chose to wear particular clothes to school. Did any of their peers' choices cause them discomfort? Did it matter to them if others perceived something different from what they intended?

By the time the discussions concluded, students themselves decided to create a "Top Ten list" about school clothing—not a dress code, but guidelines kids could use when deciding what to wear and why. Teachers knew they wouldn't always see what they hoped for. But they also saw students who had spent time and energy thinking hard about a topic that mattered, and coming to their own decisions about it.

> Adolescents are known to be rebellious. And the only way to get over that is to be in an environment where the administration isn't just as stubborn as the students. You're *shown* that you're wrong, it's not that somebody just argues with you, and doesn't allow you into school wearing the clothes you want to wear. – ADIT

This principal's approach fits right in with what students say about expressing themselves through clothes and body decoration. It's their learning at stake,
and they want to judge what does, or does not, distract them from their work.

> Provided there's no lights and fireworks coming out of the clothes, just
> let it be. It's just clothes. The more attention you give to it, the more kids
> are going to want to rebel. Teachers who feel that it's a distraction in the
> classroom can set limits in there. But if the teacher thinks that clothes are
> extremely distracting, I think the class would have to agree. – KYLIE

If they can feel like their natural selves at school, they think they will be in a
better frame of mind for learning.

> If you're going to work in an office, that's different, but we're still teenagers.
> We should wear what makes us feel comfortable. That's a big part of wanting
> to come to school, being comfortable here. If we don't get to be who we
> really are, then we're going to kind of stay closed up and we're not going
> to want to learn. – NICOLE

They treasure the individuality and creativity that their choices represent.

> Each student is different, and they are struggling to express that. That's
> one of my goals. I don't want to be looking like the person next to me,
> I want to stand out a different way. – APOCALIPSIS

> Turn on MTV, read a chicks' magazine, go to the mall and walk around and
> see what kids are wearing. If you let us express ourselves, and show our dif-
> ferent genres, then we're going to be happier in our general nature. – MIKAELA

EVERYONE NEEDS RELEASE

The music, poetry, and graffiti arts that characterize hip-hop culture often scare
adults off, particularly if they associate them with gang activities. But to

teenagers, these media serve the classic purposes of the arts, expressing a range of feelings in ways they experience as deep and powerful.

> At our school, if they see you with a graffiti sketchbook, they take it away from you. There's no reason for that, because it really is a way to express the culture, or just to get some stress off your mind. Art is like poetry, you just express your inner self, slap something on. – JOSEPH

Jose describes with admiration how one popular assistant principal at his school handled a serious community problem with graffiti, but also managed to respect what it meant to the youth who created it. This man, who heads one of ten "academies" within a large school, started by getting to know his students well enough so that he could recognize their tags painted on property in the community. Before long, he began making notes on what kids told him about gang-related activity throughout the school population.

> He hangs out with us, he's a really nice guy, and everybody talks to him. And next thing you know, I find out that he has several binders of pictures, names, nicknames, addresses, of every single student in the school that is involved in a gang. The cops know that he has all the information, and when they find graffiti they come and tell the school, and the school handles it. If you get caught you have to pay for cleaning up every little thing that you've done. – JOSE

The students might have felt betrayed, but Jose says that, on the contrary, they understood and respected the principal's actions. They recognized that he was in a position of authority and had to do something when they broke the law.

> A lot of my friends have gotten caught for graffiti because of him. And actually, they still talk to him even now, even though he was the one that gave them up! It's like when you trust somebody, it doesn't matter if they

give you up, because if you're doing something wrong, then they should do something. – JOSE

Then this principal turned his mind to providing safe and legal places for kids to paint graffiti. By taking that step, he clearly conveyed to students that he appreciated and supported their expressive talents.

> He helps them out—to keep them out of trouble, he gets them legal things to do. He put special walls up and went to the people around there and told them, there might be some kids coming and doing graffiti, don't worry about it, I'll take care of it. He owns a big house, and he tells them, I have several walls, so if you want to do something, go and be creative, I want something nice and colorful! – JOSE

Obviously, not many principals are going to want kids decorating their family homes. But schools have many possible surfaces on which students might create graffiti art. You might encourage kids to make "art cars" out of abandoned vehicles, or to festoon hallways or outbuildings with colorful murals. As they do, they will be investing their talents in making the school their own.

> If you give us space to be creative then we won't vandalize. – IAN

> Our school has a graffiti club. They let them paint the cafeteria, provided it's not offensive and you're not writing cuss words on the wall. As long as you recognize graffiti as an art, you won't get graffiti out of spite, you'll get kids trying to express themselves. – KYLIE

Perhaps even more than visual art, young people turn to music to express and release their feelings, and here again, adults often do not like or understand their choices. With digital technology, kids can bring their music everywhere, so schools continually face new decisions about what they will permit.

Students have strong opinions, for example, about whether they should be able to listen to music on headphones during quiet work periods in class. Far from distracting them, many teenagers say, music actually helps them focus.

> There's so many thoughts shooting around in my head, and half of them are worth my time and the other half aren't. When I listen to music, it helps me block out all that extra stuff and concentrate on what's relevant. I'm listening to the music, and the only thing left for my attention is what I'm doing. – KATIE

> We listen to music so much, and we learn every word of every song that comes on the radio. I sing songs and I don't even realize it. So the words don't switch our mind from one thing to another. We're able to focus without even worrying about the music in the background. – IAN

At times, music can even fire their enthusiasm for academic work.

> If I am having a hard time feeling passion about something I'm writing, music gets my blood pumping and it gets me thinking fast and passionate about something. We did a unit on the 20s, and when we first started, I wasn't really into it. I had just seen the movie "Chicago," and I was listening to the soundtrack while I was doing this one assignment, and all of a sudden it just became so much easier. – KATIE

> Different types of music put me in different moods for writing. If I want to write something happy, I put on nice music. If I want to write something angry, I'll listen maybe to rock or something hard, maybe rap. – IAN

Of course, teenagers also use music and spoken word poetry to let out their feelings in ways that have nothing to do with schoolwork. By allowing kids time and space for informal creative gatherings, adults in a school can learn a lot about students who might otherwise go unheard.

There has to be room for kids just to express themselves, and not be told to be quiet. We have kids randomly bring in their guitars on Fridays and sit around and play. For Cinco de Mayo, someone brought in a drum set and everyone was just in our little multipurpose room bonding. Don't force us to do it, don't give us a time limit, don't tell us what's appropriate and what's not, just let us say it! It lets you know that you're not alone, you're not crazy, you're not the only kid that feels that way. – CARLY

During lunchtime, you'll see people pounding on the tables, making a beat, people rapping, dancing, drawing in their sketchbooks. We could do open mike and poetry during lunch or whenever. Nothing fancy, just a regular room, people could even sit on the floor, with one chair and a mike for the poet to go. You put your feelings down on paper or into a song or by strumming the guitar strings—it helps a lot. If I feel bad and I write something down, I lose the bad feeling completely. And then I read the poem and I'm like, "Hey this is a good poem!" – JOSE

Such activities tend to spring up spontaneously in schools that consider student expression an important part of the culture. Like senior prom or the student-faculty basketball game, they become traditions that kids count on and pass along.

When you respect that, kids know it, and they are unlikely to intentionally abuse your trust. Jose, for example, described a yearly after-prom prank that the principal and students both regard as harmless fun.

All the seniors throw toilet paper all over the school, do something like that, and everybody knows that it's going to happen. The principal's already ready for it, and some of the seniors help clean it up and that's it! It's like they have an agreement with the principal or something. But it doesn't go to the extreme. – JOSE

WHEN KIDS SPEAK OUT IN PUBLIC

Students will emphatically defend a school administration they respect, but they are equally quick to criticize one that they see falling short. When they make their views public, it may especially irk a principal.

You may not appreciate opening the school newspaper's pages, for example, to find an editorial that criticizes your policy on reciting the Pledge of Allegiance, or on wearing shirts with political slogans. A cartoon that caricatures a teacher may seem inappropriate and disrespectful; a letter complaining about the guidance office may have its facts wrong.

Many principals claim the right to read the school paper before it goes to press, and insist on changes to things they find objectionable. But shooting down the ideas and work of student journalists can backfire. For one thing, the principal risks stifling kids' enthusiasm for working on the paper, where they might be learning the practices of good journalism with a faculty adviser. For another, students need to practice how to raise their voices about things they believe in, while staying within the Constitution's limits.

> It's true that high school students will not necessarily have the discretion to say what's offensive and what's not in their own newspaper. But the principal shouldn't use his right to censor the school newspaper. The reason school administrators have this power is to protect the students from [damaging] each other—not to silence the students from voicing their opinions, because that's not preparing them well for life after high school. Any action that he takes should be for the students' own good, and not for his own political purposes. – ADIT

A crackdown could also result in their producing and distributing underground newspapers, which might stray even farther from good journalism practices and ethics. Instead, student journalists need your support and trust.

> There are some really crummy schools here, and people aren't afraid to say it. When everything's out in the open, it's easier to improve the school, rather than just pretending that everything's okay. – CARLY

Just as with music and artistic expressions, a principal who respects the school newspaper provides an opportunity for learning on both sides. For you, the paper is a valuable source of real information about what's going on with kids—a way of opening and improving communication and understanding between students and adults. For kids, it is a way to learn more about the rights and responsibilities of the press.

When a controversial topic does come up, make yourself accessible to student journalists, so they can report fairly on your point of view. If you don't like what they write, don't shut them down or delay publication; they will learn more if you respond as you would to any regular newspaper. Their words may sting, but the student press is not your public relations tool.

In fact, students who express thoughtful criticism can bring credit to a school and recognition from the outside community. You can set high standards for their expression, encouraging them to raise their voices by speaking at public events, taking leadership roles in local politics, and submitting their publications for competitions outside the school. And you can help them develop new media to express themselves on the web or on radio and television.

STUDENT SPEECH, CENSORSHIP, AND COMPROMISE

- Be clear and consistent about who is in charge of review and decisions, when it comes to newspaper content, speeches, artwork, and other public displays. Trust student journalists to work through difficult decisions with the person designated to advise them.

- Make sure we're on the same page where legal rights are concerned. We should all be informed and up-to-date on what our rights and responsibilities are.

- Show interest and pride in our efforts to express ourselves. Read our newspaper, regularly and thoroughly, and not just in search of things to object to. Give us regular feedback, in positive ways. Connect us with resources and opportunities to amplify our voices in the community.

- When disagreements arise, don't necessarily call the students to your office. Instead, come have a discussion with us on neutral ground or even on our turf—our editorial office, our student lounge.

- Defend our right to tackle controversial subjects, when members of the community object and try to silence us.

What do you mean to say?

A week before the annual student talent show, two teachers come to you after they see a group of girls rehearsing their entry, a hip-hop dance. "You can't let them perform this thing," they tell you. "These are half-naked fifteen-year-olds doing bumps and grinds. It's completely inappropriate!" You agree to go look at a rehearsal, and when you see the dance you also feel uncomfortable. "Where did you learn to dance like that?" you ask one of the girls, trying to be tactful. "Oh, I take hip-hop classes at a studio downtown," she says.

You can think of several ways to respond, but you want to make sure that you are sending a clear message. What message comes across from each of the following responses?

You say to the students, "I'm sorry, but this kind of dancing is just too provocative for a school-sponsored talent show. You'll have to either tone it way down or take it out of the competition."

Your message here is: _____

_____

Benefits of this approach: _____

_____

Possible problems with this approach: _____

_____

You say to the teachers, "From what I understand, they're just doing what everybody in this dance form does. I don't like it either, but they have the right to express themselves."

Your message here is: _____

_____

Benefits of this approach: _____

_____

Possible problems with this approach: _____

_____

You say to the students, "I'm a little concerned about the response you might get from some people at the talent show. Maybe it would be good for everybody to learn more about what this dance form is all about." You suggest organizing a school assembly about hip-hop later in the year, involving other students as well as outside artists.

Your message here is: _____

_____

Benefits of this approach: _____

_____

Possible problems with this approach: _____

_____

Do you have another way you would rather respond? Write it here, explaining why you think it would work better.

_____

_____

_____

CHAPTER SIX

School should be interesting

In their leadership class at a large urban high school, Bernice and several other students began to debate why so few of their school's students went on to college. "Are we just dumber than kids at other schools?" she remembers asking. But the discussion sparked another observation as well. Compared to their friends in nearby suburbs, these students had far fewer courses and extracurricular activities that contained both interest and challenge. "Even if we could qualify for the best classes, there wasn't enough room for us," she says.

Encouraged by their teacher and by a small "action research" grant, the leadership class set out to investigate. Several months later, they had produced a half-hour video in which they interviewed their schoolmates and teachers, as well as students and faculty from nearby suburban schools. They drew out striking contrasts between the two settings—not only in their courses and activities, but in how kids felt about school and their futures. "For us, it was normal for school to be boring," Bernice said. "We didn't have good reasons to keep caring about it."

FILLED WITH CONCERNS, CURIOSITY, INTERESTS, AND AMBITIONS of their own, teenagers chafe against a system that shuts them off rather than recognizing and developing them. They know all students must learn basic skills and content knowledge, but they see that some have far greater opportunities to learn. And if classes offer only a steady diet of tedium, they would just as soon forget school and look to the media, the streets, or peer relationships for interest or stimulation.

As the school's instructional leader, the principal has a lot to do with whether students are learning in a context that engages them. Getting to that point takes some effort and imagination, and it involves dialogue with both teachers and students. But when teenagers can tell their interests really matter to adults in school, the payoff comes in higher attendance and achievement. And you are on your way to a school culture where everybody cares about what they are doing.

> There's a reason no one comes to school; there's got to be some interesting classes! The only interesting class at my old school was graphics, and that class was always full. So there was really nothing to do, ever. I have a friend who hates school, he leaves every day, but he makes sure he's back for third period just because he likes the class. – MIKAELA

> If my school gave art, then it might motivate me to show up for all my classes. – APOCALIPSIS

> I would survey the students to ask why aren't they going to class, and what would make the classes more interesting for them to go to. And then I would try to work out a more attracting curriculum for the students. – RAYNA

Students have a huge stake in the important questions of curriculum and instruction that every principal faces. If kids don't find school interesting, they don't bother to invest in it. If they do find school interesting, they give their energies freely to making it even better.

The teenagers who worked on this book suggested these ways that adults could help increase student investment in their own learning:

- Include us in determining course offerings, especially electives
- Relate academics to things we care about
- Introduce us to inspiring role models
- Connect us with opportunities for work and learning in the community
- Treat non-academic activities as important to our learning and development

WHAT MAKES US CATCH FIRE

In school and out, young people are always working on building an identity. In everything they do, they are asking themselves, "Who am I? Who do I want to be? Where am I going?" They care tremendously what others—both peers and adults—think of them and expect of them. They feel a powerful drive to think about these questions of identity, and that energy can contribute greatly to a culture of engagement in school.

> We need a class for discussion, because I have opinions about things. I know my classmates have opinions, too. We tried to start a discussion about human rights in history class this year, and the teacher shot us down and wouldn't let us finish. He said, "We have to keep to the curriculum." And so you're like, "Well, this is the curriculum! This is what I'm thinking about!" – DARIA

One school in California starts off the year by gathering new ninth-graders in small groups, where they think and write about their personal goals and values.

> At first I hated it and I would complain. But ever since then I started thinking about what do I want to do, and what do I want to be. I love math and science, even though I'm not that good at it. I have questions, and I like thinking of new ways to answer them. So I've been researching different careers in chemical engineering. – AMBER

Right from the start, Amber's inquiry into what matters to her has made her more invested in her schooling. If she gets to choose her courses, she can explore her identity even further.

You can build on that momentum by organizing academics so they connect to students' interests, while still allowing kids the room to change and grow.

One way of changing students' attitude is showing them how a high school education will relate to things that pique their interest. So if a student were to be interested in music, they would be taught a curriculum based upon music. Still teaching the same standards, but with an emphasis on how your education can be used toward music or construction or medicine, all fields. Not necessarily saying that's what they want their career to be in the end, but whatever they're interested in at the moment. – JAQUAN

For me it's paramedics and firefighting, I think that's the coolest stuff. What if school had a paramedic course, and intermediate and advanced training? The dropout rate would be so much less, you could ask anybody. – CRAIG

You want the opportunity to make choices, but you also want to be able to change your mind. It's hard when they ask you to sign up for a particular academy when you're just starting out, like in ninth grade. In my case, I chose technology and engineering. But I didn't really know what these subjects were or how long they'd interest me. – TROY

Students realize that the state decides the broad outlines of the high school curriculum. But courses of high interest to students can also fulfill state or district requirements for core academic skills. Many students identify strongly with popular culture and media, for example, and a course on media literacy could meet a requirement for language arts, social studies, or both.

I think every school should have a media class—not necessarily just running the school newspaper, but really understanding and interpreting the media, studying the media bias, studying photographs, things like that. – KYLIE

The courses that most attract students are often those that use a theme or question to explore a range of subjects.

Here's how a hip-hop class would help us: With the rap, it would help us in literature and writing. Dancing, it would be a health class. Drawing, it's an art class. And all that put together will ease our mind and make us better at learning, instead of spending our time in class drawing sketches or something while we're supposed to be doing our work. — JOSE

BUILD ON THE THINGS THAT MATTER

Students feel more eager to expand their learning if they can start from a point where they have confidence. Jerry, for example, already likes carpentry and hip-hop music, and he sees how his academic skills could build from those interests.

Carpenters might have to measure something that could be in a shape of a rhombus, and if you had a music class, kids could communicate better with the rhymes. — JERRY

One interest often leads to another. A ninth-grade project in which Amber explored her English ancestry, for example, led her into science and art.

We integrated a lot of things into it, like history, which I love, and Darwin. And I did a History Day project on teaching creation science versus religion in public schools. And I got to study a lot of philosophy, which I like a lot. Also I oil painted an interpretation of a metaphor in a book we were reading in philosophy, *Sophie's World*, where the world is like a white rabbit coming out of the top of the universe. It all carried together. — AMBER

Many principals understandably worry about whether their students will do well on standardized city and state tests if their coursework focuses on things that interest them. Kids say that the risk can work the other way around—that they will tune out completely if the material does not connect to their interests. In his early years at a large New York City high school, Vance had that experience.

> There was a lot of pressure on the teachers to just teach to the state test,
> because if we didn't pass it they didn't keep their jobs or something.
> They still cared about the work, but every time there was a spark, or some-
> thing would start to happen—you could feel it, you could feel kids getting
> interested—the teachers felt bad, they felt sad, like, "Oh we have to go
> back to the text." We weren't the only ones that were disappointed, they
> were disappointed, too. – VANCE

But after he transferred to a school that had obtained a waiver from the state tests, Vance did much better. His new school offered courses combining rich academic content with high student interest, with titles like "Constitutional Law" or "Chemical Puzzles" or "Fiction of the Immigrant Experience." Its curriculum set a tone of challenge and depth that respected students' capacity to take on hard questions that mattered to them.

> The pressure was off, basically, for passing this big test that decided your
> future. It was more about your life. That one test didn't make your life—
> just learning the curriculum, that helped with your life. – VANCE

Elective courses are particularly important in holding students' interest and keeping them learning, and teenagers are keenly aware of the inequities among schools in this area. Luke, who goes to a large urban high school, and Rebecca, who attends a well-financed suburban school, have very different course offerings.

> We basically have the bare necessities as far as classes go: math, science,
> English, etc. Maybe if you could get the students and parents united to
> say, "We want this program, put pressure on the district to give money to
> establish it," then we would be more interested in attending school, and
> do more. – LUKE

> We have a lot of really cool electives. We have a multicultural course, we have a Literature of War and a Nazi Genocide course, we have journalism, mass media, creative writing, a symposium for history, we have Vietnam, the American TV age, intro to behavioral sciences... – REBECCA

Asiya grew up in an urban neighborhood but went to elementary school in a nearby suburb, under the city's voluntary busing program. After eighth grade, tired of being among so few students of color, she transferred to a high school closer to home. She liked a lot of things about her new school, but the contrast in the courses it offered took her aback.

> A lot of people don't notice; they just think that's how school is. But I was so disappointed—like, "Where's my keyboarding and my photography? I want to dance!" – ASIYA

Teenagers know they can't control all the decisions about what courses the school offers and how they are taught. But they say that if those who decide would listen seriously to their thoughts, students would feel more like partners in their schooling.

> Talk to us about the classes that we want to take, not just the ones you want to give. We know what we need to take, so respect us by asking us what is on our mind or how we feel. Don't just give us orders; listen to what we have to say. – JOSE

> If my school didn't require all students to take a dead language by the third year, maybe they wouldn't all cheat and sleep through class. – OSCAR

> I find myself making sock puppets for an English class in twelfth grade, which is not something that reaffirms my faith in high school. – ADIT

WAYS TO HELP MAKE OUR COURSES MORE INTERESTING

- Get teachers in different departments to talk to each other about the curriculum.
- Encourage faculty members to pair up to teach cross-disciplinary courses.
- Hire teachers who are qualified in more than one subject area.
- Emphasize projects that give us hands-on practice in using key concepts, knowledge, and skills.

CLASSROOMS THAT TREAT US AS PEOPLE

Course selection is not the only route to a school where young people are interested in learning. Your attitudes about what goes on in the classroom have a big effect on whether students feel like partners or like prisoners there.

When your faculty connects with the identity questions that underlie every teenager's behavior, the classroom can take on an entirely new tone, which respects the issues individual students might be struggling with.

Starr prides herself on having an independent nature, for instance. She particularly dislikes asking questions that make her look less confident in front of her friends and teachers.

> My adviser was also one of my English teachers, so she knew a lot about the classes I was taking and about who I am. She worked with me on my personal level—that helped me a lot academically. I could start to mix the social thing with the academic thing. I talk a lot and I know a lot of

people, so now I can do a survey, for example. I can incorporate my own personal life into the things I do for work. – STARR

Like Starr's adviser, teachers who know their students well can make powerful connections between academic subjects and the things kids worry and care about.

> The smart teachers find the smallest reason why you might need math, or you might need science. If you have asthma, you're worrying about your lungs, your pulmonaries. That's something you know—you're having trouble with your breathing. Maybe your mom has diabetes, or your dad has a bad heart. And so we listen, even begrudgingly, because it makes sense.
> – VANCE

Sometimes, adults can find those connections just by staying alert to contemporary youth culture. Anders came to high school with a bias against history and English courses, but by his junior year he found a teacher who made them matter.

> I can't sit down and listen to a teacher talk about what happened centuries ago—like I care. But right now I have a teacher who can relate to kids, and that helps. They relate things that happened in the past to things that happen now that matter to me, and they know what those things are. – ANDERS

Introducing students to inspiring role models is another way to foster their interest in academics and show them the value of school.

> Have college alumni who are very successful, like professors, come and talk to students. Like, "Hey, you don't have to stay on the streets so you can get a nice car, you don't have to live with your mama so you can earn a living." Some kids want to be rappers or producers, so get a college alumni who is a producer. Show what he did to stay away from the burdens around him, like drugs and violence, and how he has really prospered because of his

education and his knowledge. If you want a life, education is a good way for you to be happy. — TISHA

I'd love to meet female politicians, 'cause that's what I aspire to. If someone like that came to give a lecture, she could encourage us in areas that students are lacking in, and it would end up very inspirational. A lot of students would come by choice. — ELEONORA

Adults, too, have something to learn, and young people may be able to help them. That recognition can give a class a sense of excitement and purpose, as teachers stretch their own skills and knowledge alongside students.

They're not always experts. One of our teachers started the robotics course because he also wanted to learn about robotics. He learned with us. He would go to extra classes so he could teach us new stuff. We could, like, learn off of him and he could learn off of us. — ANDERS

As principal, you can signal to everyone in your school that you want and expect adults to explore connections with students and their lives. Perhaps you will find ways within the school day for teachers to get to know their students better. You might share with the faculty good examples of coursework that connects with student interests. And when teachers try new ways to spark student learning, you can celebrate their results.

LEARNING THROUGH HANDS-ON PROJECTS

High school students feel much more interest in learning when the curriculum includes hands-on projects, not just lectures and paper-and-pencil exercises.

Think back the last time you read something. Do you remember that easier than something you just did, like when you helped someone cook something? You can't remember something someone told you as well as something that you just did. You are trying to apply something to yourself. If you just have lectures, after two weeks of break you just totally forget everything. Maybe if there were more hands-on experiences, kids wouldn't be forgetting what they learned. – MONICA

Still, they recognize that they need practice in the underlying academic competencies to pull off a project that really matters to them. As a project in physics class, Charles and his classmates built a sail-powered car.

Someone can throw all this information at you, but if you're not willing to practice it, it's not worth it no matter how great the school or the teacher is. When I learned the traditional formulas it got kind of boring. But doing the project at the same time, I began to link the formulas with the actual construction. It inspired me to get deeper and deeper into the book. I was craving more, because I saw how some of these formulas could really boost the performance of the car. And the more you practice all different types of these math problems, the more naturally it comes. We need the balance of both. – CHARLES

Monica describes a biology project that extended into her math and humanities classes.

We're growing eucalyptus to see if eucalyptus extract stops the germination of different seeds like oat, rye, and diachondria. In math class, we're doing statistics for that experiment and learning to use Excel so we can make a graph of our results. Through that I learned about statistics, which I can use in other things I do. In humanities, we're writing a paper about our project, and the writing is easier because I actually did it, I'm not just reporting what someone else did. You could do the experiment, but if you don't have your statistics or results, or you can't read them, then the project is worthless. Or if you can prove something but not explain it in writing, then what's the point of doing it? – MONICA

Students are not trying to avoid academic challenge when they ask for more interesting classes. They want work that will start with what they know and care about, then build on it in exciting ways that stretch their thinking and leave them wanting more. As the school's instructional leader, you can support teachers in developing these active, inquiry-based lessons that will draw teenagers into new understanding of important concepts.

You can also show teachers, district administrators, parents, and the community just how much students learn when adults take their interests seriously and include them in the curriculum. Did a science class produce a light show as the culminating project of a unit on optics? You can point out in public the concepts and skills kids had to master along the way, as well as the habits of persistence and teamwork that it required of them.

THE COMMUNITY CAN TEACH US

When high school students have the chance to work directly with adults in the community, their interest and engagement goes up markedly. Whether this happens in service learning projects or internships, kids appreciate the chance to develop their skills and knowledge in a setting outside of school.

> Every Wednesday, we go out for the entire day and do community service, and it's really made a big difference to me. In our building we have Early Head Start, where moms drop their babies off, and I go down there and help them take care of the babies. That's really made me want to go to school on Wednesdays, getting to loosen up and have a little bit of fun, not be so severe all the time. – KATIE

The summer before her junior year, Monica helped a local community center set up a teen center. The next year, her school helped her turn her new interest into an internship opportunity.

> I helped with payroll and little things like filing and making phone calls that they needed. I wasn't really thinking about it till after the summer was over, but when I started to do my resume again, I started to think about that stuff. A lot of skills I learned at school I had to use—like habits of mind, collaboration, communication, how to see stuff through other people's perspectives. – MONICA

Quan and a classmate had an internship at a nearby science park, surveying the public about a virtual reality game that showed the effects of smoking cigarettes. Their project benefited the park's management, but it also stretched him personally, he says.

> My friend and I would ask what they think, gather the data and put it into the computer, then analyze the data and see the trend. I learned how to be more outgoing. I'm a quiet type and with this my communication skills really boosted up. It's important to know how to work with others in the field. – QUAN

Ryan's internship at a scientific research institute led him into an independent exploration of new academic areas.

> I was making a mid-oceanic ridge database. Where the lava comes out of the ocean floor and the plates expand, there's a line in between the spreading centers, where they've slipped. You have to define them with the end points and the azimuth, and then they have a name. I didn't know a lot about geology, so I went and got some books and read them, and now I know a lot more. Then we had a bunch of raw data from a digitizing tablet

that collects points to get latitude and longitude off a map, and I had to learn a new programming language to format the data. I wouldn't have learned those things if I hadn't needed to. – RYAN

After Jon learned the rudiments of web design in a high school class, he was hooked, buying books and attending outside seminars to find out more. Noticing his new passion, his school set up an internship for him at the nearby university.

I met a multimedia guy at the university, and we kept constant contact, talking about what I could do. Now he is my mentor at the language acquisition resource center there. I finished my project for them early, in two weeks, making a presentation tool for him. It's interesting—I'm in high school, and this other guy there who's studying for his masters is asking me things, saying, "You know a lot more than I do!" – JON

Often, student projects directly benefit the school. Kiel made a short video documentary in his junior year about his school's internship program. Because the school would actually use it to acquaint students, parents, and employers with their roles and responsibilities, the project seemed more worthwhile to him.

I never would have thought to do a project like that. I had never done videos before, but once I got involved, I cared about it being a quality project. I didn't want to put [only] half of myself into something that was going to be seen by hundreds of people at conferences. I cared about the video because it was an important thing, and the school had a lot riding on it. Because it was important to them I gave it my best effort. – KIEL

WE'RE LEARNING ALL DAY

Academic classes do not necessarily rank at the top of what keeps students interested in school.

People tend to forget that school is more than what happens in the classroom. It's for the extracurriculars, like sports, that some kids come to school at all. Sometimes it's the only place we get to feel like we are good at something. – MARISOL

Learning is important, but there has to be other stuff, like dance and drama and singing, 'cause it's boring when you're just in school studying. – Karina

We just made a mural painting program, where we got to draw and paint on the walls, so that's a great thing that I'm doing. The principal helped organize it with a couple of artists, so now we have the funding. Programs like music and art are very important, so that we have another way to stimulate our minds, other than academics. – APOCALIPSIS

Not only do students often care more about activities outside of class, but they also learn and grow a lot from taking part in them. In fact, studies have shown that participation in extracurricular activities is an even better predictor of success after high school than academic grades or standardized test scores. In some cases, the activities involve skills at least as useful as those taught in academic courses.

Our student store brings in tens of thousands of dollars a year—many adults don't run operations that can bring in that kind of money year after year! And the fact that we can do it is something that should really be encouraged and highlighted. It really is beautiful that students are having fiscal responsibility and more students should be brought into that. – ADIT

Especially when they do not involve competition, clubs and activities foster a tone of inclusion that often comes as a relief to students.

I know it sounds crazy, but at our school we started a cheese club this year. Sure, it's about cheese, but it's also about creating a small place where kids feel equal to each other, where people know your name, where no one is advanced or not advanced. – TRACY

Every school should have a debate team, and not just formal debates where everyone comes in a suit and tie, but something that really gets everyone into the debate, and something that kids are passionate about. – KYLIE

And because students often initiate such activities, they have a stronger investment in them from the start.

Performing arts shouldn't just be like the marching band, the orchestra. Our school has this little unofficial garage band that comes in and plays guitar, and they don't charge for their performances. Don't schedule them, don't print out invitations and what to wear to them, just let kids get together and play along. It's more real, and it takes a lot of the tension out of the environment. – KYLIE

But it's not always easy for students to get an activity off the ground. The principal's response can make all the difference, they say.

I was trying to plan an end-of-the-year trip for the eighth graders last year, and I needed help from the principal for busing and stuff. I went to his office so many times, and every time, "He's in a meeting, he's not here right now," and I couldn't set a date to see him. It made me feel like he didn't really care. – ASIYA

A lot of the kids in my school wanted to open a stepping program, after school, and two senior girls were going to teach it. We went to the principal and as soon as possible he helped us open it, and a lot of students were going and it was a great activity. That made me have more respect about the principal, because he cared and listened to us, and he took it very seriously. – ENKA

A principal's interest and encouragement concerning extracurricular activities lets kids know that you respect the things they care about. Whether your support is psychological, financial, or logistical, it pays off in the increased investment that students feel in their school.

> Take activities that show promise, like the Black Students League, and incorporate it into the school so that it's just as valid as the third-period German class. Unlike a German class, unlike a history class, extracurriculars are things that students are demonstrating a voluntary interest in. And if you make that interest a piece of the school's community, you have successfully incorporated those students into the school, and you've made them have a vested interest in the affairs of your school. – ADIT

Looking at students' ideas of how to make school more interesting, you might think about how you feel about the tasks that confront you at work every day. Just like adults, high school students don't expect their workday to include only experiences they enjoy. But they do need a sense of agency, purpose, and meaning in what they do with their time and energy. And whenever you link your own goals with that one, you will come out with a stronger school culture.

> Why shouldn't the administration and students team up to do something based on the unique talents or interests of the students? It's not only that you're celebrating your kids, and the students are representing their school. It's another effort in that same vein to make the school not just a solid institution that the students butt their heads against, but a dynamic entity. – ADIT

Could we do that in school?

Here are some things that students often ask for to make school more interesting:

- Write a play and put it on
- Take a camping trip with their class
- Have a class in hip-hop
- Take a day to walk around the city in small groups
- Make a web page for a class they're taking
- Read fantasy novels in English class

In the space provided, add any ideas that you have heard in your school:

_____

_____

_____

What structures already exist in your school that might possibly support these ideas?

- ☐ After-school activities or clubs
- ☐ Volunteers from the community
- ☐ Non-teaching staff from the school
- ☐ Elective courses during the school day
- ☐ Academic courses that already exist
- ☐ Other_____

_____

_____

Now choose one of the ideas students have suggested. If you were to carry that idea forward, what next steps would you have to take? Check all that apply from the list that follows:

- ☐ I could approach an adult within the school who might be interested in supporting such an activity.
- ☐ I could ask parents and guardians if they might be interested in supporting such an activity.
- ☐ I could approach an adult from the larger community who might be interested in supporting such an activity.
- ☐ I could draw positive attention to teachers who are already trying out ideas like this.
- ☐ I could bring students and teachers together to talk about coursework.
- ☐ I myself could lead an activity like this.

Other _____

_____

_____

_____

For the idea you chose, what obstacles do you think you would encounter if you tried to make it happen? _____

_____

_____

Who would you need to involve in order to overcome these obstacles?

_____

_____

_____

CHAPTER SEVEN

Our bargain in the classroom

Angela's tenth-grade biology teacher started out on the wrong foot with the class, and by midterm Angela calls the course "completely useless." One day the teacher will launch into a tirade at the students, she says, the next day he will let them goof off during a lab exercise. And although almost nobody understands the material, students have given up asking questions because the teacher's mood is so unpredictable. All the sophomores hate the class and spend the period doing anything but paying attention. They've written off the course, says Angela, but nobody expects any change.

Angela thinks the principal should do something about it, but she says that when kids complain about a teacher, it can get them into a lot of trouble. "People with power can use it to get back at you," she says. "When there's a problem with teachers, it should be recorded exactly what happened and when, and it should also be kept between the student and the principal."

G OOD TEACHERS CAN FILL STUDENTS WITH THE ENERGY that comes when one has important things to contribute and accomplish. For teenagers heading toward adulthood, this can make all the difference in capturing their interest and pushing them toward new ways of thinking. But when the opposite happens, students like Angela get discouraged, tune out, or act up. The teacher's job gets even harder, and a downward spiral begins.

You can help both teachers and students break out of that spiral, by reminding them of the bargain teenagers make with teachers when they come to school. Here's how they describe what's fair:

IF YOU WILL . . .	THEN WE WILL . . .
Show you know and care about the material	Believe the material can be important for us to learn
Treat us as smart and capable of challenging work	Feel respected and rise to the challenge of demanding work
Allow us increasing independence but agree with us on clear expectations	Learn to act responsibly on our own, though we will sometimes make mistakes in the process
Model how to act when you or we make mistakes	Learn to take intellectual risks; learn to make amends when we behave badly
Show respect for our differences and individual styles	Let you limit some of our freedoms in the interest of the group
Keep private anything personal we tell you	Trust you with information that could help you teach us better

Your school probably has plenty of consequences, from bad grades to suspension, that follow when students don't carry out their side of that bargain. But when teachers don't carry out their part, very often no one will notice except students.

The lapse could be happening with inexperienced teachers, or with those who feel burned out or don't know or care much about the material. But it also might happen because nobody in the school—not the principal, not the teachers, not even the students—has ever made the nature of the bargain clear.

In situations like those Angela described, students feel indignant. They know something is not fair and they want to right the balance. But they may not completely trust that you will take the bargain seriously and back them up.

No matter why the balance in the classroom goes wrong, word usually drifts back to the principal. Either students complain directly, or their defiant behavior gets them sent to the office for discipline. Here, perhaps more than at any other time, students like Angela are depending on you to act as a role model.

If a teacher has let the students down, you can show them how adults work out such a problem in a respectful way. If students have behaved badly, you can help them see where they went wrong and then make amends without losing their dignity.

In the process, they will see that you regard their learning as your top priority. Once they trust you on that, they won't need to act out their frustration in the classroom. They will know that they can always come to you.

> It's very frustrating if you can't really go any higher than the teachers. When everything's out in the open, it's easier to improve the school, rather than just pretending that everything's okay. — CARLY

Students who worked on this book had this to say about how you could help everyone hold up the bargain teachers and students make in the classroom:

- **Put good teaching first**
- **Take seriously our feedback about teachers**
- **Work to improve teachers' skills, not just ours**
- **Help us resolve problems with our teachers respectfully**

WE NEED GOOD TEACHERS

To teenagers, few things matter more in school than a knowledgeable, challenging, imaginative, and caring teacher. And they know one when they see one.

> If you feel very strongly about what you teach, we'll see that—no matter if

you're a balding white guy with glasses coming into the toughest neighborhood in the Bronx. That's your strength—it's not the fact that you can beat us up or expel us, it's the fact you feel so strongly about us. A lot of teachers think that students only respect one kind of power. But we know there's different types of strength—there's the strength of the heart, of believing in yourself. — VANCE

Kids can tell whether their teachers feel like committed professionals or are simply putting in their time.

First of all, the teachers gotta love their job. If they love their job, then they're going to do what they have to do to see that the kids succeed in life. — DEANDRE

If the teachers aren't happy, if they're unsatisfied with their contract or anything, they're just not going to be doing the greatest job. As much as they want to teach the kids, they're going to take it out on them without wanting to. — OSCAR

They notice the things a teacher does that help them succeed in class.

A school worth going to is one where the teachers have positive attitudes. Where they care. Where if I fail a test, they take me aside and tell me to come and get tutored with a couple of other kids. Where they are willing to adjust their teaching styles and make them as diverse as their students. — TRACY

Every teacher does not teach the same, they realize, just as every student does not learn alike.

If they want to teach a certain way, allow them to teach that way, because that's the way they're going to teach best. If they want to use certain materials to teach, let them use those materials, because those are the materials that they're going to use best. — JAQUAN

But when a teacher comes across as ill-prepared, bored, or disdainful, adolescents will protest by tuning out, acting out, or failing.

> In the beginning she was being nice but then she started yelling, "You do this 'cause I say so." The principal never asked us, he was just like, "Why don't you respect her?" And we had reasons, 'cause she never respected us either. — ENKA

OUR FEEDBACK SHOULD MATTER

Enka's comment that "the principal never asked us" speaks to the heart of the matter. When a principal goes to the source to find out how teachers are doing, kids get a clear message that you care about their learning.

> The principal should check up the same on students and teachers. Say a student was having problems in a certain subject and the principal asked what's wrong, and the student said, "I'm trying to understand, but I just don't." Then the principal can go to the teacher and say, "There's probably some other people who don't understand, and maybe you should try to teach in another way." — ASIYA

> A principal should go into classes and observe what is the teacher doing. And make sure that they're going spontaneously. Don't tell the teacher, because the teacher will make up a whole new different plan how they run the class. — RAYNA

You can tell a lot just by chatting informally with students about how their classes are going.

> Go around and converse with the students, just a salutation walking down the halls, or while they're eating lunch. The principal can ask, "What are the good things in this class that the teacher is doing, what can be improved?"

If the students feel comfortable with the principal, they can talk about problems with their classes. — RAYNA

A simple evaluation form at the end of a course can also provide valuable input, to both teachers and principals.

If a teacher really wants to get to their students, then they not only have to hear that little voice in their head saying "This is right," but they also need to hear it from the students. — JAQUAN

The students know a lot, and we have issues. It's not just the students causing the problems; lots of times it is the teacher. There was a math teacher for years, just sitting in front of the class, and she wouldn't answer anyone's questions. And the principal actually noticed lots of complaints and had a talk with her and let her go. That was great, because the principal could see that okay, we have a problem, it's time to fix it. — RAYNA

WHAT TO ASK US ABOUT OUR TEACHERS

- Did the teacher offer us any extra help during school or after school?
- Did the teacher have prepared lesson plans?
- Did the teacher encourage our participation in the classroom?
- Is the teacher passionate about the subject taught?
- Was the teacher organized? Did he or she lose our papers or anything?
- Was the teacher fair to us or did he or she show bias?
- Did the teacher know our names? Did he or she have a relationship with each of us?

TEACHERS CAN LEARN, TOO

Students keep a very close eye on everything that adults do in school. So by helping teachers to learn more about what they teach and how, you set a powerful example. It's part of the bargain: When teachers show they know and care about the material, kids will believe that it's important.

You also send a message by making continuous teacher learning part of the business of school. Here are some things that students notice:

- When teachers attend a workshop, you ask them to report out not just to their colleagues, but to students, too.

- When you visit a class to observe it, you show your interest in teaching and learning by asking questions about what the class is doing.

- When you talk about teaching and learning in faculty meetings, you sometimes arrange for students to participate in part of the session.

- When teachers miss class for professional development, you find substitute teachers who know and care about the students and the material.

The word will get around among students when you take teacher learning and student learning just as seriously. They don't expect their teachers to know everything, or to do everything right. But they will feel the balance tipping toward fairness.

A BALANCE OF POWER

When they have issues to work out with their teachers, students often need the principal to act as a liaison.

> Some students are not heard as much as they want to be, and some teachers still treat them as if they were still in second grade. And that's not fair at all, because you're trying to get a point across and they're not paying attention

to you. If it gets to that point, have a teacher, student, and administrator conference, so the administrator can be the liaison between the student and the teacher. — DEANDRE

But for this to happen, students must trust that you will listen with an open mind to what they have to say.

> In one of my science classes, one of the teachers actually called one of the students in the class a slut. That kind of hit her right there, but she was too scared to go tell the principal. — MARVIN

> When students get sent to the principal's office, they shouldn't be like, "Okay, this is your punishment." They should ask them what happened and get their point of view. I realize that students do get out of line, but sometimes teachers can be wrong in what they say and do. The principal should discuss it with the student and the teacher separately, and then have them come together and talk it out, without getting into an argument. — NICOLE

Many students fear the consequences if they stand up for themselves.

> It's easy for teachers to retaliate, using grades, or getting you in trouble for random things. — CARLY

> My friend bent down to grab something on the ground and her underwear showed a little bit, and the teacher pulled her off to the side and was like saying, "Your mom needs to buy you different underwear, you can't be wearing that kind," totally making her feel uncomfortable in class. We talked to the principal about it, but the teacher was kind of mean to her the rest of the year. — NICOLE

By gathering information from both sides and maintaining an impartial and respectful attitude, the principal can model how to approach difficult situations where an imbalance of power exists.

One time I got kicked out of my world history class, because I had yelled at the teacher. I confronted him because I had heard that he was talking about me behind my back. And I told our assistant principal the truth. It's that kind of honesty and trust that you build as time goes on, as you get to know him. – JOSEPH

And once students see that adults hear and respect their points of view, they are willing to help solve the problems that come up.

We had a history teacher that wanted to do things straight from the book, reading every single day. And some of the students didn't think that that was the best way to learn. The teacher went to the principal, and said there's a disciplinary problem, the students are always arguing. So the students and the teacher and the principal, we came up with this little compromise: We were going to read, but then do other activities besides reading, watch different movies and things. – LETICIA

WHEN TEACHERS FALL SHORT

- Take students' feedback seriously. Their comments can help teachers do their job better. Tailor professional development to bolster teachers' skills in areas where they need improvement.

- Bring students into the hiring process, both formally and informally. Encourage them to participate on the committee that reviews resumes and interviews candidates. Ask prospective teachers to teach a sample lesson, and invite students to comment on it.

- In areas where classroom teachers fall short, provide additional supports to students. Ask community support for after-school tutorials or enrichment.

Observing a teacher through students' eyes

When you observe teachers in the classroom, you are probably evaluating their performance according to well-established criteria. But students also have criteria for what makes a good teacher.

How many of the items that students consider important also show up on your own observation checklist for classroom instruction?

WHAT STUDENTS LOOK FOR IN A TEACHER	ON MY LIST ALREADY	NOT ON MY LIST
Knows us and seems to like us.		
Cares passionately about the subject.		
Knows the subject well.		
Takes our questions seriously.		
Cares about what we think.		
Doesn't just teach one way.		
Doesn't play favorites.		
Doesn't blame us when we don't know.		
Gives us another chance when we mess up.		
Keeps enough order so we can learn.		

What seems different about what students look for, compared with what you look for when you observe a teacher in the classroom?

_____

_____

_____

What seems the same?

_____

_____

_____

After reading what students have to say in this book, is there anything you would want to add or subtract from your own teacher observation checklist?

_____

_____

_____

In evaluating your own performance, do you have new thoughts about what might be important to the students in your school?

_____

_____

_____

_____

_____

_____

_____

_____

_____

_____

Students as Allies
In Improving Their Schools

BY BARBARA CERVONE

W HAT IF TEACHERS AND STUDENTS became steady allies rather than frequent adversaries? What would it take for students to become stakeholders not just in their own success but also in that of their teachers and schools?

With support from MetLife Foundation, What Kids Can Do (WKCD) explored these questions in an initiative called "Students as Allies," which offers a pragmatic and achievable example for readers who hope to put into practice the ideas set forth by students in this book.*

In Chicago, Houston, Oakland, Philadelphia, and St. Louis, WKCD collaborated with teams of students and teachers organized by a local nonprofit intermediary. The work in each city included several parts: helping students conduct survey research about their own schools, supporting dialogue and constructive action around the research results, and nurturing youth leadership along the way.

As the first step in creating this initiative, MetLife Foundation and What Kids Can Do together selected the five Students as Allies sites. Then WKCD identified local partners—typically a school reform, youth development, or community group—each with unique strengths and relationships to schools in their district. Universities also served as critical collaborators, providing assistance in all phases of the research. (For a list of participants, see page 142.)

Local partners varied in how they assembled their project teams, composed of

---

* For more about Students as Allies, go to www.whatkidscando.org/studentsasallies.

a corps of students supported by teachers and other adults. In St. Louis and Houston, for instance, schools applied to the local partner to participate in the project, then each selected school gathered its own research team. In Oakland, students in newly formed leadership classes in three high schools, along with their teachers, formed a joint research team. In Chicago, student volunteers from four high schools also worked jointly; and in Philadelphia, student researchers were drawn from a summer youth program run by Temple University.

NURTURING NONTRADITIONAL STUDENT LEADERS

"I think that every student who participated is going to be an example to their school. Students will look up to them and hopefully listen and try to understand and support them. Maybe this will make school a better place for all of us." — ERMARDIA, ST. LOUIS

From the start, Students as Allies aimed to enlist students who were not recognized leaders in their schools. Though student teams did also include these traditional leaders, we believed that engaging students who did not stand out in academic or social settings would enrich the participatory research process. We hoped that their questions—and the students of whom they asked them— would bring out voices that otherwise might go unheard.

In some cases, this inclusiveness happened naturally. Teachers in the Greater Houston Area Writing Project (the backbone of the work in that city) wove the initiative into one or more of their regular classes, turning every student in the class into a participant. In Philadelphia, the student researchers came from Temple University's "Youth Voices" summer program, which works with roughly ninety teens from the city's poorest neighborhoods and schools.

When composing the research teams in St. Louis, however, teachers purposefully thought about all the various cliques that made up their student body, then recruited students who reflected this diversity. At one school, teachers enlisted a male student who always seemed on the leading edge of trouble in the cafeteria and another whose black attire, body piercing, and diffidence screamed "off limits."

In Oakland, all of the ninety student participants were enrolled in a special class designed to cultivate nontraditional student leaders. Its curriculum examined obstacles to learning in high schools where poverty, alienation, and violence sap hope, and many of the students brought this consciousness to the project. That shaped the issues covered in their surveys: what happened too often (student profanity or class disruptions), and what didn't happen enough (being greeted in the morning by administrators or studying with friends outside school). Later, it also fueled their impatience with moving findings to action.

In all the Students as Allies sites, reaching out to students who seemed unlikely leaders gave participants the chance to learn important leadership skills. Lessons in teambuilding and communication skills intertwined with survey design and analysis in the training students received. These enduring benefits to individual students count among the initiative's strongest contributions.

PARTICIPATORY RESEARCH

"Adult researchers have written all these reports about which students are failing and why. It's time students became the studiers and not just the studied. We might even teach the professionals a few things." – JOSE, HOUSTON

When invited to carry out their own research on their schools, then supported in that task, students can ask questions and collect answers as rigorously as any adults. They may also ask questions that do not occur to academic researchers and use more youth-friendly language, increasing the likelihood that fellow students will respond thoughtfully. Our experience with Students as Allies gave ample evidence of that.

Our research process

We launched our research collaborative by studying recent national surveys of teachers and students conducted by MetLife. We identified areas where knowing the thoughts of students and teachers might help students become actors in improving their schools: school climate, student-teacher relationships, teaching styles, academic expectations, safety and discipline, student voice, and improving student learning, among others. Having agreed that a survey would be our primary research tool, we then drafted questions tied to these areas and circulated them among the student research teams in all five sites. We encouraged students and teachers to reword, collapse, or omit questions as they saw fit and to add questions specific to their own school. We cared more that students learn survey design and own their research than that they keep questions identical so as to generalize the results across teams.

The student research teams took this invitation to heart, sharpening questions that seemed ambiguous and engaging classmates in focused discussions to determine what needed investigating within a school. The team at one St. Louis school, for example, conducted seventy-five interviews before drafting and finalizing the school-specific part of their survey.

In the end we had almost as many different surveys as schools participating. All included, however, a common core of questions within and across sites, along with questions particular to each team. That blend would yield both data that could represent the whole project and data whose meaning resided within a specific school.

More than 6,350 students completed surveys, and in St. Louis and Chicago 446 teachers did so as well. (Houston teachers, surveyed in a later effort, numbered over 100.) Student teams determined whom they would survey within their school, aiming for a representative sample, and administered surveys during class time.

The schools, by and large, were medium-sized to large urban high schools facing numerous challenges; few would end up on a district's "high performing" list.

What we found

Predictably, student researchers uncovered both positive and troubling news.

Much good will and intentions

Despite constant headlines about schools in crisis, our results showed an abundance of good will, even at schools described as failing. Eighty-nine percent of the students polled across the five sites said, "I really want to learn," and 83 percent said they participated regularly in class. Eighty-seven percent said they respected most of their teachers; 84 percent thought their teachers respected them.

TIPS FROM STUDENT RESEARCHERS

- Remember that you only get answers to the questions you ask. Also, be sure to ask the same question in different ways.

- Be careful how you word your questions. Poor questions get poor answers.

- Survey teachers along with students, especially on the same issues. We found big differences in each group's experience of school.

- Explain to students and teachers in advance of administering the survey what it involves and why it's important. Remind students that it's not a test—nor a joke. Tell them how you'll use the results.

- Use SurveyMonkey.com. Students and teachers can answer surveys online and get organized data back immediately.

When asked to grade their teachers, 84 percent gave their teachers an A or B on "knowing their subject well"; 76 percent graded teachers with an A or B on "being well organized" and "believing all children can learn."

Teachers expressed even more upbeat attitudes. Ninety-three percent of those surveyed agreed that other teachers at their school were committed to teaching and doing what is best for students; 87 percent believed their school curriculum challenged students. Eighty-nine percent thought that teachers at their school respected all races and cultures, and 81 percent said their colleagues had high expectations for students.

Concerns about respect for students

The survey also surfaced a number of concerns. Students split down the middle on whether they believed the majority of teachers at their school regarded students as individuals and did not stereotype them. While 52 percent gave their teachers an A or B on teaching students according to their individual needs and abilities, 17 percent gave them a D or F.

Students were equally divided on the fairness of their school's discipline policy—or more precisely, whether it was applied uniformly across the student body. At one Oakland high school, 57 percent of the students said the administration did a good job of "posting and clarifying school rules," but only 38 percent thought the administration "enforced school rules evenly."

Only half of all students surveyed agreed that faculty and administrators valued what they have to say. This was perhaps our most consistent finding, rarely wavering more than a few percentage points from school to school and site to site.

Among students who reported they had considered dropping out of school (18 percent), 58 percent cited not getting along with their teachers as the biggest factor. Only a quarter picked bullying or school safety.

Discrepancies in views of student-teacher relations

The survey turned up troubling discrepancies in how students and teachers view their interactions with each other. Two-thirds of the students said that their teachers did not understand them or their life outside school. More than a quarter of the students surveyed said that there was not a single adult in their school whom they felt they could approach with a problem.

Survey results revealed a striking gap between how frequently students and teachers report talking one-on-one with each other about various issues. In Chicago, 27 percent of students said their teachers often talked to them one-on-one about active classroom participation and good academic performance; 80 percent of the teachers, though, said they brought up these subjects often in one-on-one conversations with students. While only 33 percent of the students said their teachers often explained to them individually how to complete a homework assignment, 70 percent of the teachers reported having this conversation frequently with individual students. The numbers in St. Louis told a parallel story.

What could help students do better

In several sites, students asked peers how much various items would support their learning. The list included real-world applications, more one-on-one attention from teachers, more challenging classes, and more parent or guardian involvement. Real-world learning won the most votes from students; 53 percent said it would "help a lot." One-third of students agreed that being able to take textbooks home would help their studies a lot.

Variations among sites

Student responses varied considerably across cities on several issues. For example, only 46 percent of the Chicago students and 51 percent of Oakland students

St. Louis students and teachers who report often or very often talking one-on-one about . . .	Students (N=4,460)	Teachers (N=358)	Percentage Difference
Class behavior	19.0%	40.4%	21.4%
Plans for college or work after high school	32.4%	58.8%	26.2%
Academic performance	28.6%	66.5%	37.9%
Completing homework assignments	24.9%	67.0%	42.1%
Interests and things important to students	29.6%	77.7%	48.1%

thought their school was safe. In Houston and St. Louis, however, 68 and 83 percent, respectively, believed their school was safe. While 84 percent of the St. Louis students said their teachers were respectful of students, the percentage dropped to 68 in Oakland. More Chicago students than in any other site (39 percent) said their school's curriculum was not challenging.

School-specific findings

We found the questions students asked in the school-specific portion of their surveys as interesting as their answers. They reveal profound differences in culture and opportunity that distinguish schools not just in different parts of the country but within miles of each other.

In Houston, for example, academic pressure topped the list of student concerns in one of the district's most rigorous high schools, where half the students are enrolled in honors classes. The survey students created had no fewer than forty-five questions on the subject, some alarming: "Bellaire's competitive culture encourages cheating" (60 percent agreed) or "When I am sick, I come to school anyway because I will have too much make-up work if I stay home" (82 percent agreed).

By contrast, three very different issues received special billing on the students' survey at Houston's Lee High School, where a once largely white, middle-class student body has given way to immigrant students. (Over 40 percent speak limited English.) These included replacing tennis courts that no one uses with a basketball court (80 percent were in favor); cleaning up the bathrooms (96 percent agreed, but only 52 percent were willing to help clean them); and taking teachers on guided tours of students' neighborhoods (opinion split on this idea).

Taken together, the school-specific questions also showed how much students cared about their school and what they valued. They asked, among other things:

- Are our teachers passionate about what they do?
- Do our counselors know us?
- Is it easy to make new friends at our school?
- Are we getting the computer instruction we need to succeed?
- Should our school have an open campus? A school mural? A school store?
- What items should get top priority in the school budget?
- When it comes to diversity, does our school practice what it preaches?

THOUGHTFUL DIALOGUE

"We hope this report sparks important conversations among students, teachers, and administrators across our city. We must all talk if our schools are to improve."
– CHICAGO'S FINAL STUDENTS AS ALLIES REPORT, APRIL 2004

Among adult researchers, the process of gathering data and weaving it into a written report sometimes stands in for energetic dialogue about the findings. With our student researchers, nobody could mistake one for the other. They were eager, even impatient, to generate conversations about their survey results with those who mattered most: their teachers, administrators, and classmates.

Analyzing our results

The conversations began with students making sense of the data they had collected. Within their schools, they analyzed the results from their school-specific surveys; at special meetings of teams from across schools, they dissected their citywide results.

Students debated what might account for a particular finding. Why, the team at one Chicago high school wondered, did 83 percent of the teachers believe their school was safe, but only 32 percent of students? Another Chicago team explored why 35 percent of the students surveyed said they had considered dropping out of school, but only 9 percent had ever talked to a teacher about it.

Students also asked hard questions about what made a finding reassuring or troubling, and what they hoped to see if, as one student put it, "things in our school were in good working order." In St. Louis, for example, 57 percent of the 4,460 students surveyed agreed that they were involved in school decision-making and that their teachers valued their opinions. Reversing the result, however, students judged as unacceptable the 43 percent of students who felt they had little or no voice. "It should be more like 25 percent," they agreed, reasoning that for probably a quarter of the students in any school, voice may not be a concern.

With regard to a "sense of belonging," the St. Louis students set the bar higher still. Seventy-nine percent agreed with the statement "I feel I belong at my school, that I'm accepted and liked." For some of the student researchers, the fact that one-fifth of the students felt they didn't belong was disturbing. "I know it sounds unrealistic," one student said, "but if we really mean no child left behind, then every student needs to feel they matter in a school."

Public presentations

In all five Students as Allies sites, student research teams presented their findings at public summits that brought together students, teachers, and administrators. Each summit followed its own script.

The largest, in Houston, gathered 400 students and teachers from fifteen of the city's twenty-four comprehensive high schools for a day of presentations, workshops, and discussions. Student teams shared their research using familiar presentation tools like flip charts and PowerPoint but also through skits, video, and hip-hop poetry.

The smallest meeting, in Chicago, engaged all sixty-five participants in interactive exercises. In one, participants indicated their level of agreement with a specific survey question by moving to specified areas of the room—"strongly agrees" in one corner, "somewhat disagrees" in another, and so on. Student facilitators then invited participants from each corner to explain their choices, opening up spirited discussion.

At Philadelphia's summit, students presented their findings to a panel composed of a district administrator, a funder, a university researcher, and a community activist. "You have real concrete data here," said the district administrator, "and we must make it part of our planning." The university researcher challenged the students to explore the root causes underlying the problems they had surfaced. "You need more analysis to know where to look for leverage and allies," he advised.

In St. Louis, student-teacher teams and university and community partners gathered to compare notes in "mini-summits" every three months. At the fourth and final meeting, students and faculty from other St. Louis high schools joined the conversation, and in roundtable discussions queried each research team in depth about their work. Later, a dozen of the student guests took part in a "fishbowl" exercise in which they talked among themselves about what they had learned, while the Students As Allies research teams listened in.

SAMPLE ANALYSIS

(from student researchers at Young Women's Leadership Charter School, Chicago)

Statement:

Sixty-five percent of the teachers in our survey said that not having enough time to get to know students was a minimal problem, while 64 percent of the students said there were no teachers, or at most one, with whom they can talk about personal issues.

Hypotheses: What may explain this disconnect?

- Many teachers don't value getting to know their students. Students pick this up in a teacher's body language, their attitude, the things they don't say, as much as what they do say. A cycle of mutual avoidance sets in.

- Many teachers may feel that they shouldn't deal with student issues that are someone else's responsibility, like a social worker. If it's not in their area of expertise, there's not a lot of incentive to take on the responsibility. Getting to know students well doesn't show up in a teacher's paycheck.

- Many teachers have a habit of dismissing personal issues students bring up as irrelevant to the subject. This gives students the impression that a teacher is unapproachable. It creates a mental barrier between students and teachers.

- Some teachers may be afraid to let down the student-teacher barrier for fear that it will result in the student bringing false accusations against the teacher.

Oakland's summit convened student, teacher, and community activists from throughout the city, in addition to the Students as Allies research teams (from three of the city's six comprehensive high schools). As well as students presenting their research, the agenda included workshops to build concrete skills in areas like youth organizing and college access.

Classroom discussions

Public meetings like these offer crucial venues for students to make their voices heard. However, as one of our student researchers commented, "what really truly counts is when we can talk about these issues in class, with the teachers and students we mix with daily, where the conversation can make an immediate difference."

Many teachers in the project carved out time in their classrooms for just such conversations. To help them along, we provided discussion prompts and exercises, drawing from the questions WKCD author Kathleen Cushman used with forty students to create *Fires in the Bathroom: Advice for Teachers from High School Students* (The New Press, 2003).

For example, students and teachers explored the ways that teachers unknowingly encourage or discourage students. They asked, "How does a teacher give little signals that she expects you to try hard and do well? That she doesn't expect you to? That she thinks you are smart, or not?"

They critiqued teaching strategies in which students are invited to be more active, asking, "What do you like or dislike about group work, hands-on activities, projects and presentations, and why? If they're not working, what could teachers do to make them work better?"

They explored tensions between students and teachers that sometimes disrupt classrooms. "What does it feel like to be in a class where there's a lot of tension?" they asked. "How does a teacher know when a student has disrespected her— or vice versa? How can the teacher fix the situation?"

WHAT MAKES A TEACHER WORTH PAYING ATTENTION TO?

(from students at Chavez High School, Houston)

WHEN the teacher interacts with the students and isn't afraid of a challenge, she is always there for her students

WHEN they are caring, funny, and inspiring

WHEN they don't put you down or make you look bad in front of other people, when they stay on your level and actually talk to you, when they don't call on you when they know you don't know the answer

WHEN they believe I can do my best if I just put my mind to it and not be lazy

WHEN they let me know exactly what I have to do and when I'm doing a good job

WHEN they relate schoolwork to real life problems

WHEN they give us a lot of work but make sure we understand it before they move on

WHEN they don't scream at us, when they always try their best to explain whatever you need help on

WHEN they don't judge you before they get to know you, when they make you comfortable because they talk about their life so that it seems like you know them

WHEN they use a variety of methods for learning, when they teach one-on-one if necessary, when they put effort into their students' learning

They learned more about each other's strengths. In one exercise, students and teachers listed everything about which they knew a lot—regardless of whether they learned it in school or out—along with who had helped them learn it. As they shared their lists, they discovered unknown talents in others, and gained a heightened awareness of the ways and places in which learning occurs.

Of all the participants, Houston students and teachers in particular invested in classroom discussions like these as part of their Students as Allies work. Many read and discussed *Fires in the Bathroom* as a classroom text. Later teachers there spoke glowingly of the ripple effects:

- "For many teachers, it was a surprise to hear how strongly students yearn for good teachers and recognize good teaching when they see it, how they long to learn, and how annoyed they are by students who don't take learning seriously."

- "In our small school academy there is much change. Remarkably, a lot of it is within the faculty. We are communicating better, there is more of a bond, and we see each other as faculty more regularly. I can't pinpoint what about the project has made this happen, but it has. There's simply a lot more attention being paid to relationships within the school than ever before."

- "Students have told us, in ways we never understood, how horrible and wasteful school suspensions can be. They have underscored the things we'd prefer not to see: how easily kids can obtain drugs within school walls, how much time gets wasted in class without real learning, how dropping out or getting pregnant seem like legitimate alternatives to students who have fallen far behind. Things must change, they tell us."

TAKING ACTION

"For once, I hope my students believe this is possibly going to bring about real changes in our school. Otherwise, they could care less. The real work starts where the data leaves off." – TEACHER, HOUSTON

Even for seasoned researchers and activists, translating data into change can be enormously difficult. For our student teams, taking action on the issues flagged by their research required that they learn additional new skills. First, they had to decide what they would tackle, picking issues that are both meaningful and "winnable." Second, they had to figure out where their leverage lay with respect to these issues. Third, they had to cultivate allies; and fourth, to maintain their seriousness of purpose as they asked others to take them seriously.

In Chicago and Oakland, where individual school teams also joined together to form a larger cross-school team, the initial action step was to engage district administration in considering their findings. Students in Oakland met with the state-appointed administrator who now oversees the district, his chief of staff, and the director of high schools in a discussion that lasted two hours. A group of students also filmed the meeting, adding to it other footage they took as part of a video documentary of the project; the film (called "Holla' Back!") aired on local public television. In addition, the state-appointed administrator attended the students' public summit, where conversation continued about how to tackle their recommendations from the data.

In Houston, students chipped away at small, discrete items raised in their school-specific surveys. At Lee High School, for example, where refurbishing the school bathrooms stirred strong feelings, students wrote a proposal and won funds from a local foundation to overhaul the bathrooms, contingent on students helping to keep them clean. At Bellaire High School, students and teachers began taking a hard look at healthy ways to relieve academic pressure, like improving coordination among teachers with respect to scheduling major assignments and frank discussions about cheating. At another Houston school, the principal established a regular time each day for students to drop by to talk; with input from students, the vice principals also reworked disciplinary polices and reconsidering the dress code.

The action taken in St. Louis stood out for the systematic approach taken by its student-teacher teams. Each team selected and developed a plan of attack for one or more issues that met both the "meaningful" and "winnable" criteria. Remedies were small but immediately tangible; as they identified an issue, students had to answer the question, "What do you want to see, hear, and feel [as a result of this action]?"

Much of this energy focused on improving student-teacher relationships, and the strategies were plentiful. They include shortening classes by a few minutes to create twenty to thirty minutes each morning for students and teachers to meet; creating a student-coordinated "teacher of the month" award; facilitating email communication among teachers and students; and developing a program of student-teacher symposiums on topics of mutual concern. At one school, teachers posted in the faculty room a chart listing the name and grade of every student. They asked teachers to check off the students with whom they had at least a modest relationship in order to identify those students whom faculty barely knew—and then to do something about it.

As much as any school, St. Louis's Webster Grove High School showed what is possible when will and data join forces. First, the student-teacher team flagged the most troubling survey items (like teachers feeling frustrated and unappreciated in their jobs, or students complaining about teachers playing favorites); then they grouped the items in themes. Later they organized and held a weekend retreat that brought together forty students, fifteen teachers, and fifteen community members and parents to draw up strategies that would forcibly respond to the identified concerns.

Some of the actions were surprisingly easy or inexpensive: putting up more student work on the walls, creating a peer tutoring program, allowing students to pursue independent study, encouraging teachers to stand at their classroom door to greet entering students. One teacher commented, "It's the small things that add up, especially when they are noticeable, and make people feel hopeful."

The Webster Grove retreat, however, also produced what many would consider a large decision: The administration agreed to make students part of all hiring decisions at the school. Students also will regularly evaluate teachers, providing written feedback on both the effectiveness of their teaching and their relationships with students.

Lea Garcia, a student on the Webster Grove Students as Allies team, ticked off her accomplishments: "I've talked with the principal in early morning meetings. I've discussed the situation with fellow students. I've discussed the survey and how we can condense it. I've gotten valid opinions and concerns from my peers. I've learned about some things that need to be changed in our school. I've taken on a leadership role in the process."

We would add to her list one last item: This student has helped breathe renewed hope and purpose into her school.

STUDENT AS ALLIES PROJECTS

Chicago, Illinois
Partner: Cross City Campaign for Urban School Reform
University: Chicago Consortium on School Research
High schools: Dyett Academic Center, Orr, Roosevelt, and the Young Women's
Leadership Charter School

Houston, Texas
Partners: Houston A+ Challenge and the Greater Houston Area Writing Project
University: University of Houston at Clear Lake
High schools: Bellaire, Chavez, Furr, Lee, Madison, Reagan, and Scarborough

Oakland, California
Partners: Oakland Unified School District, along with Youth Engaged in
Leadership and Learning (YELL), Youth Together, and Youth in Focus
University: John W. Gardner Center at Stanford University
High schools: Oakland Tech, McClymonds, Skyline

Philadelphia, Pennsylvania
Partner: University Community Collaborative of Philadelphia at Temple University
High schools: No direct school partners

St. Louis, Missouri
Partner: CharacterPlus / Cooperating School Districts of St. Louis
University: University of Missouri–St. Louis
High schools: Francis Howell, Lindbergh, Perryville, Rockwood Summit,
Webster Groves, Wentzville Holt

Index

What Kids Can Do, Inc. (WKCD) is a national not-for-profit organization founded in 2001 for the purpose of making public the voices and views of adolescents. On its website (www.whatkidscando.org), WKCD documents young people's lives, learning, and work, and their partnerships with adults both in and out of school. WKCD also collaborates with students around the country on books, curricula, and research to expand current views of what constitutes challenging learning and achievement.